Alive In Christ

Alive In Christ

The Christian Life As Seen In The Ark Of The Covenant

Charles W. Price

Marshall Pickering
An Imprint of HarperCollinsPublishers

Marshall Pickering is an Imprint of
HarperCollins*Religious*
Part of HarperCollins*Publishers*
77–85 Fulham Palace Road, London W6 8JB

First published in Great Britain
in 1990 by Marshall Pickering

1   3   5   7   9   10   8   6   4   2

Copyright © 1990 and 1994 Charles W. Price

Charles W. Price asserts the moral right to be
identified as the author of this work

A catalogue record for this book is
available from the British Library

ISBN 0 551 02892 0

Printed and bound in Great Britain by
HarperCollinsManufacturing Glasgow

Contents

Introduction

I once thought of calling this book *Raiding The Lost Ark!*
Steven Spielberg's blockbusting film of a similar name
created a lot of interest and perpetuated some of the myth
and mystery which surrounds the Ark of the Covenant
that God told Moses to build. For ever after, until its
destruction, the Ark was the place where God could be
approached. Although much of this book is a look into
the Ark of the Covenant, it is not primarily about the Ark,
but about the role of Jesus Christ in the life of the
Christian, something graphically portrayed by the Ark
and its contents. The Ark was the place where God and
man made contact, where his purpose was made evident
and his power apparent. Three things were placed in the
Ark which each portray a particular ingredient of the
Christian life now available under the New Covenant
through the indwelling presence of Jesus Christ in the
Christian.

Although this book is intended as a book of biblical
exposition, my concern is not with the Bible itself, but
with the life that is to be discovered as a result of all true
biblical exposition: the life of Jesus Christ. It is not only
his life as history, but his life as contemporary experience
that is the concern of Scripture. The only gift God has to
give us is the gift of his Son, for 'this life is in his Son. He
who has the Son has life'. By his Holy Spirit, it is the Lord
Jesus Christ who reproduces in us the character he once

demonstrated in his own body. Christ-likeness is the inevitable consequence of true Christianity, not by imitation of him, but by allowing Christ to be himself in us. This is the goal of the Christian life and the source from which all else of value derives.

Charles Price

1: When All You Can Do Is Push!

On one of my frequent absences from home the grass on our lawn was in need of cutting. We had recently purchased a new motor mower, which my wife Hilary had seen me use several times. Knowing I would not be back for several days, and the fine weather was not likely to last until then, she decided to mow the grass. The mower was fairly solid, with rotary blades, roller and petrol motor weighing down on the machine. She started the engine, which automatically began to turn the blades in its stationary position, and then began to push. It was really hard work! To get any movement took almost all her strength, but determined as she was, she applied all her might and with her body against the mower at a forty-five degree angle she gave it everything she had until after two lengths of the lawn she was exhausted!

This was very confusing. She had seen me walking up and down the lawn behind the mower, apparently effortlessly. Although she knew I was stronger than she was, she also knew the difference wasn't as great as this! In frustration and anger she grabbed hold of the handle to give the machine a good shake and in so doing caught the clutch lever and engaged it. Suddenly the mower took off across the lawn under its own power, cutting the grass in its path with Hilary flying out behind it almost horizontal to the ground! What a marvellous difference!

How frustrating to find yourself manually operating something designed to run on its own power! And how wonderfully liberating to discover after a long, hard, tiring struggle that there are resources at your disposal you knew nothing about. This has been the personal experience of many people right through history. They have tried with the utmost sincerity and dedication to do for God what only God himself could do for them. There was no fault in their zeal or failure in their enthusiasm. They just did not know or appropriate the indwelling presence of God himself, as the only One who can provide what it takes to accomplish his will. When out of despair and exhaustion they find Christ to be alive, and alive in them, the discovery has been revolutionary.

There can never be any significant progress in the Christian life until a fundamental discovery has been made and appropriated: 'It is no longer I who live but Christ who lives in me'. (Galatians 2:20)

'The Strength You Have'

There is a man in the Bible whose back was against the wall. He, along with the people around him, was intimidated, oppressed and defeated by an enemy who refused to slacken its oppression, much less to quit. His name was Gideon. The Lord came and spoke to him one day, and said: 'The Lord is with you, mighty warrior'. (Judges 6:12) Gideon was totally unimpressed. 'If the Lord is with us, why has everything gone wrong?' he asked, and began to recite the troubles and misfortunes of his nation, whose past history was full of dramatic stories of God's intervention on their behalf, but whose present experience was only one of misery and defeat. All they knew of liberty were stories parents might tell their children around the fire before they went to bed at night, but they bore no resemblance to the present realities. The oppressive Mideonite neighbours were constantly on their backs, reducing them to poverty and ridicule. 'If the Lord is with us, why is all this happening?' he asked. It was a good question! If this was more than some meaningless theological statement, more than a dead statement in a dead creed, where was the evidence of God acting on their behalf? The answer God gave was to be a great surprise.

The Lord turned to him and said 'Go in the strength you have and save Israel out of Midian's hand'. That was a revelation to Gideon, '*the strength you have*'. Whatever strength God was speaking about it was not something he was to receive, but something he already had. Gideon asked the obvious question, 'How can I save Israel? My clan is the weakest in Manasseh, and I am the least in my family'. In other words, 'You say I have strength, yet I am the least and the weakest. How can you tell me to go in the strength I have, it is totally inadequate'.

The Lord answered Gideon: 'I will be with you'. This was the explanation. God himself was his strength. He was not speaking of some kind of strength that might come to Gideon in packaged form. Although he already knew God, Gideon had not been counting upon God, he had been counting only upon himself. But now he was to make a great discovery. The Authorized Version gives an alternative translation in its margin, of the expression 'the Lord came upon Gideon' stating most beautifully, 'The Lord clothed himself with Gideon'. (Judges 6:34) The simple yet most profound discovery any Christian can make is that God himself is our strength. He does not simply give it to us, nor does he teach us techniques for producing it, but it is *himself*! Fail to realise that and live in the good of it, and the Christian life will be like pushing a heavy lawnmower across the lawn, when all the time the engine waits only to be engaged!

As I write this it is less than a week since a student at

11

a well known Bible College in North America came to me at the end of an address I had given and said 'I decided only this morning that I am going to quit this college, give up my plans for going into Christian ministry and maybe even quit the Christian life. My experience has been totally frustrating, and Christianity has been about as exciting as pushing a bus up a hill. This morning you have shown me something I have missed all these years. I now have the answer.'

The principles I had shared with the students that morning are very simple and certainly not new. The Christian life is not a technique or a 'style', it is exclusively the consequence of a relationship that allows God to be God within a person's life. It is the indwelling Spirit of Christ himself who makes the Christian life 'tick'.

Peter: When Tears Lead To Triumph

The Bible never glamorizes its leading characters and it may be encouraging for us to discover we rarely come unstuck in a way that is original. The apostle Peter pushed his lawnmower across the grass for a long time. Of the twelve apostles, chosen and called by the Lord Jesus Christ to be with him during the three years of his ministry, we would almost certainly have noticed Peter first, and not only have noticed him, but admired him too. Whenever something was happening, he was around – active, opinionated and utterly committed to doing the best thing. Even when Jesus told his disciples for the first time that he must go to Jerusalem and die, 'Peter took him aside and began to rebuke him. "Never Lord" he said. "This shall never happen to you" '. (Matthew 16:22) Jesus rebuked him for this. Nevertheless, despite his not having a clue as to what he was really saying, his motive was to protect the interests of Jesus as he best understood them, and it was admirable.

Peter was his most loyal and enthusiastic supporter. If he could do something for Jesus that would further the cause there would be no need to look elsewhere. Peter would do it. The night of Jesus' arrest Peter confirmed his unswerving loyalty to him by declaring, 'Even if all fall away on account of you, I never will', and when told that he would disown Jesus three times before the morning broke and the cock crew, Peter was emphatic: 'Even if I have to die with you, I will never disown you'. (Matthew 26:33–35) If the Roman authorities had to place four crosses on Calvary, with Peter on the fourth, Jesus need not doubt that Peter would be right there with him, to die alongside him. Wouldn't you have been impressed with that? There is no reason to believe that Peter believed himself to be anything but sincere and genuine in his commitment and loyalty. He loved Jesus Christ with all his heart. He was his most loyal friend, his best advocate and his most enthusiastic supporter.

Within a few hours Jesus had been arrested and led away for trial. Peter had resisted the arrest, and in the process cut off the ear of Malchus, the High Priest's servant. Most of the other disciples fled, though Peter, keeping a distance, followed him to the house of the High Priest. In those early-morning hours, Peter was questioned three times by three different people as to his association with Jesus, and three times he considered it safer to deny any knowledge of him. On the final occasion, 'he began to call down curses on himself and he swore to them, "I don't know the man" '.

Having got himself off the hook for the third time in those early brief hours of the day, Peter's sense of relief was abruptly shattered when across the courtyard of the High Priest's home was heard the crowing of a rooster. Like a knife going into his heart, 'Peter remembered the words Jesus had spoken . . . and he went outside and wept bitterly'.(Matthew 26:74–75)

13

Have you ever wept bitterly over your own repeated failure? Your sincerity has never been wanting, but you were somehow unable to carry it through to the end. You have known what is right, but rarely seem able to produce it in your own behaviour or experience. You feel you could despair of ever being different, even wondering if you ought to quit.

Jesus later summed up Peter's dilemma, 'The spirit is willing but the body is weak'. (Matthew 26:41) What in his spirit was admirable, could not find its translation into action, and in the realization of that fact, Peter faced up to his own moral and spiritual bankruptcy. A few days later, Jesus was risen from the dead, but Peter, despite the euphoria of the resurrection and still aware of his own weakness and failure announced to the other disciples: 'I am going fishing'. (John 21:3) I am not sure if I read this correctly, but three years before he had been called from his fishing, and had left everything behind him to follow Jesus. Now he is going back! He perhaps thought there was little point in doing otherwise. He had only proved he was not dependable. His actions could not match his words. What good was a willing spirit if his body was weak? It might be better all round if he slipped back to his old life. He would always love Jesus. He would never forget him. He would treasure for the rest of his life the memories of the time he had spent in his company as a disciple. He would always be interested in what happened to the others. But he was burned out. He had been exposed under pressure for what he was really like. He was humiliated. At least he could fish. There was always work that he could do. Several of the others joined him, and they fished all night but it was a waste of time. They caught nothing!

Early next morning a stranger stood on the shore. They did not know who it was. He asked them if they had any fish, and telling him they had none he instructed them,

14

'Throw your nets on the right side of the boat and you will find some'. (John 21:6 ff.) They did so, and were unable to haul in their nets, so great was the catch of fish. John was in the boat with Peter. Something in his mind was ringing a loud bell. This seemed a repetition of an event three years ago. The very day that Peter, Andrew, James and John had been called by Jesus to leave everything and follow him, they had been fishing all night and caught nothing. Then Jesus came along the shore and told them to cast the net on the other side of the boat. They had done so and hauled in such a catch that both boats began to sink. Peter had jumped from the boat and fallen at the feet of Jesus and said 'Go away from me Lord, for I am a sinful man.' (Luke 5:1–11) This had been the time of their call by Jesus. He invited them to leave everything and follow him. They had never again gone back to fishing, from then on they had been 'fishers of men'.

John, no doubt recalling all of this, and giving voice to his suspicions said to Peter, 'It is the Lord.' (John 21:7) When Peter heard this his heart was stirred. He leapt from the boat and made his way to the shore. It was Jesus! He had made them breakfast over a fire of burning coals. The others in the boat quickly joined them, and when they finished eating, Jesus asked Peter a question. In the light of his recent past it must have seemed a very pointed, if not embarrassing, even humiliating question. 'Simon, son of John, do you truly love me more than these?'. I think the question must have cut deep into his soul. This was only the third meeting of Jesus with his disciples since the resurrection. Only a few days before, at Jesus' most vulnerable moment, Peter had cursed and sworn his denial of ever knowing him, rather than claim to be his friend. How could he now claim to love him? Yet Peter knew his own heart, and despite all that had happened he had only one honest answer: ' "Yes Lord" ', he said, 'You know that I love you'. Jesus said, ' "Feed my lambs." ' The question, its answer, and the commission of Jesus were repeated three times.

Peter discovered something very wonderful that morning. Jesus never, ever gives up on failures! He never even penalizes them. He knows their hearts, and he knew Peter to be a failure before Peter ever did. The Lord had not been shocked by Peter's denials, only Peter had been shocked. He is not shocked by your failures for you will never be a bigger failure than he already knows you to be! But Jesus was not commissioning Peter back into his failure. He was not just inviting him to have another go at it! In the opening chapter of Acts, Luke records 'On one occasion when he had been eating with them, he gave them this command: "Do not leave Jerusalem but wait for the gift my Father promised, which you have heard me speak about." ' (Acts 1:4) I find it interesting that it was while eating with them, he gave this command. I wonder if it was the breakfast of bread and fish he himself had prepared for them by Galilee? I wonder if he has commissioned Peter, knowing Peter has finally realized he could not carry it through alone, and so he reassures him he must attempt nothing until the gift of the Holy Spirit has been given? I think that may be so.

For Peter, the morning of tears as the cock crew on the fateful morning that Jesus died, preceded and made possible a new morning of joy seven weeks later. It was at nine o'clock in the morning on the Day of Pentecost, that the Holy Spirit was poured out on all who were waiting to receive him. Peter stood to address the crowd who had come together, looking for an explanation of the great events that accompanied the outpouring of the Holy Spirit. In the intervening seven weeks, Peter, stripped of his self-confidence and self-sufficiency, had been commissioned by Jesus to 'feed my sheep'. He stood that morning in new strength, he spoke with new authority and the city of Jerusalem was turned upside down. When later a lame beggar was healed at the temple gate, and a crowd gathered around, Peter declared to them the simple facts of the case: 'Why do you stare at us as if by our own power or godliness we made this man walk? . . . It is Jesus . . . that has given this complete healing to him, as you can all see.' (Acts 3:12–16) The explanation for what he did was no longer 'Peter' but 'Jesus'. He learned it, not in a classroom, or even from the lips of Jesus who had declared in his hearing 'Without me you can do nothing,' (John 15:5) but it had begun to make sense as the truth dawned through the bitter tears of his failure, the morning the rooster crowed, and he knew he was at the end of himself.

2: God In A Box – The Ark Of The Covenant

For some years as a Christian, I had a mentality that saw God as being *up there* somewhere, and I was *down here*! I was on his side, he had forgiven my sins, he would take me to heaven, I had joined his fan club and he was the one for whom I now lived. But I did not know that I could not live the Christian life! I thought I was supposed to try my hardest and do my best, and was only filled with remorse over my obvious and abysmal failure. But, as we have seen to be true in Peter, this sense of failure became the source of wonderful discovery. It is the presence of God himself *within me* that gives the ability to live the Christian life. This does not put us in to a neutral stance where we became a puppet in the hand of God, but it is in his energy and his strength alone that we can live and survive.

This has always been God's purpose and strategy in the world. His actual presence in his people, and his working amongst his people has been the source of everything that has ever been accomplished of lasting value. This is true of the Old Testament era as well as the Christian era. It is never what we do for God that is the criteria, but what God does for us. This does not lead to a passivity on our part, as we shall discover, but will result in our living under an authority and in a strength that is not our own.

This raises a fundamental question. How do you know

that God is with you? I don't mean in the general sense of God being in all places all of the time, and therefore with you in all places at all times. In that sense we are never out of his presence. 'Where can I go from your Spirit? Where can I flee from your presence? If I go up to the heavens, you are there; if I make my bed in the depths, you are there. If I rise on the wings of the dawn, if I settle on the far side of the sea, even there your hand will guide me, your right hand will hold me fast.' (Psalm 139:7–10) In that sense we can never be out of his presence. I am not speaking of his presence with us in that general sense, but of his activity on our behalf.

God promised Moses, 'My presence will go with you, and I will give you rest.' (Exodus 33:14) This is what would distinguish Israel from all the other people on the face of the earth. This 'presence' is God in action, doing things on their behalf. There were other times when God declared that he would 'cut people off from his presence.' (*See* Leviticus 22:3; 2 Kings 23:27; Jeremiah 7:15; 23:39) This did not mean they would be banished to a place where God was not, but that from then on they would simply function on their own. They would not know God's power, his wisdom, his guidance or his strength.

In a period of the Old Testament, God's presence was tangibly amongst his people in the form of a wooden box, overlaid with gold – the ark of the covenant. When God gave Moses instructions to build the ark, which would be the most important piece of furniture in the tabernacle, being placed in the Most Holy Place, he made this statement: 'There . . . I will meet with you.' (Exodus 25:22) If you wanted to meet with God and for him to meet with you, it would be at the ark.

The ark was kept in the Most Holy Place under the most stringent regulations. However, once in a while, the ark was taken from the tabernacle and marvellous things occurred wherever it was carried.

The Ark In The Jordan

When the people crossed the Jordan River to enter Canaan, God gave clear instructions to Joshua regarding the ark. (*See* Joshua 3–4) The priests were to carry it to the Jordan, and the people were to move out from their positions and follow it at a distance of not less than a thousand yards. When they reached the edge of the Jordan River, the priests carrying the ark were told to go and stand in the river, and at that point the water stopped flowing and a path opened through the river so that the people could cross over. During this time the priests who carried the ark remained standing in the middle of the Jordan, but, as soon as the last person was through to the other side, they stepped up out of the river and it began to flow normally again. This was a miraculous occurrence. People have from time to time given alternative explanations for the opening of the Red Sea forty years earlier as the Israelites left Egypt, but the Jordan is specifically stated as being in flood. The role of the ark was crucial in this event, but it was not the ark that brought about the miracle. Joshua had declared: ''Consecrate yourselves, for tomorrow *the Lord will do amazing things among you,*' and later 'This is how you will know that the *living God* is among you.' It was God who performed the miracle. The ark was the symbol of his presence amongst them and of his power on their behalf, but it was God alone who was responsible.

The Ark In Jericho

Having crossed Jordan the first big obstacle to taking Canaan was Jericho. It was described as 'tightly shut up. No one went out and no one came in.' (*See* Joshua 6) God again gave clear instructions in which the ark figured prominently. The Israelites were to march around the city once each day for six days. On the seventh day they were to march around seven times. At the head of the procession were seven priests with rams' horns and immediately behind them was to be carried the ark of the covenant. On the seventh day, on the seventh time around the city the people were to shout. This they did, the walls collapsed, they invaded the city and captured it.

The carrying of the ark was a crucial part of the proceedings, but it was not the ark that brought down the city walls. It was not a magic box. *God* brought down the walls. He had said to Joshua before they started marching 'See, I *have* delivered Jericho into your hands.' Joshua had declared on the seventh day: 'Shout! For *the Lord* has given you the city.' The ark was the symbol of God's presence and of his power, but it was God himself who performed the miracle, and God alone.

The Ark At Mount Ebal

Having got into the land of Canaan and enjoyed their first few victories over the enemy, the nation met on Mount Ebal to renew the covenant God had made with Moses. (*See* Joshua 8) The whole nation, aliens and citizens alike, the elders, officials, judges, men, women and children all gathered on either side of the ark of the covenant. Joshua engraved on stone again the law God had given Moses on Mount Sinai, and then he read aloud all the instructions, commands, the blessings and the curses that had been given to Moses. We are not given details of how the people responded, though I imagine it was very much as at a later time when Joshua renewed the covenant at Shechem. (*See* Joshua 24) On that occasion Joshua challenged the people to 'Choose for yourselves this day whom you will serve.' The people responded: 'We will serve the Lord.' Standing around the ark to make their covenant, it was not to the ark they made their allegiance, but to God. The ark only represented God.

In some strange way, this ark symbolized all that God was, and all that he intended to do for his people. They were to treat the ark as though it were God. If they were to meet God, they were to meet him at the ark. This is why it was taken into the Jordan. This is why God told them to take it around the city walls of Jericho. It represented, in a physical tangible form, the presence of God. This made it both dangerous, as some were to discover to their great cost, and powerful.

The Ark As Israel's God

Many years later when in combat with the Philistines, the Israelites brought the ark of the covenant into the camp. 'When the ark of the Lord's covenant came into the camp, all Israel raised such a great shout that the ground shook. Hearing the uproar, the Philistines asked, "What's all this shouting in the Hebrew camp?" When they learned that the ark of the Lord had come into the camp, the Philistines were afraid. "A god has come into the camp," they said. "We're in trouble! Nothing like this has ever happened before. Woe to us! Who will deliver us from the hand of these mighty gods? They are the gods who struck the Egyptians with all kinds of plagues in the desert. Be strong, Philistines! Be men, or you will be subject to the Hebrews as they have been to you. Be men and fight!" ' (1 Samuel 4:5–9) Motivated by this rallying call, they took on Israel, fought them and actually beat them. It is not relevant to discuss the reasons for that at this stage, though as a result they captured the ark of the covenant and took it back into Philistine territory. The particular point from this narrative is that the Philistines identified the ark itself as a god, and more specifically as the god responsible for all of Israel's victories in their history. That is understandable. The ark was not God and in that sense

22

they were wrong. However the ark represented God, and to that extent there was substance to their fear.

The Philistines actually beat the Israelites on this occasion because the Israelites had made the same mistake. Having just been defeated by the Philistines they had retreated with their tails between their legs and said, 'Let us bring the ark of the Lord's covenant from Shiloh, so that *it* may go with us and save us from the hand of our enemies.' (1 Samuel 4:3) Instead of recognizing what Joshua had recognized, it was the Lord who would take them over Jordan and it was the Lord who would give them Jericho, they substituted the ark for God himself and declared that '*it*' would save them. And of course '*it*' didn't! Only '*He*' could! The moment we substitute God himself with even a legitimate means by which he works, God moves out. Anything God may bless as an expression of himself, he curses when it becomes a substitute for himself. That is what happened in this instance.

But there is more to this box — the ark as given to Moses. We shall discover it to be a beautiful picture of the Lord Jesus Christ. If we want to meet God, we must meet him in his Son. If we want to know God's strength, his power or his wisdom, we receive them in Christ. 'His divine power has given us everything we need for life and godliness through our knowledge of him.' (2 Peter 1:3) Outside of Christ, God has nothing to offer us of true substance. This is why it is relevant and will be helpful for us to examine the ark of the covenant, as it is valuable for us in general, to examine the Old Testament scriptures.

The Old Testament: The Story Of Christ

It will be helpful at this stage to explain our approach to the Old Testament. The Old Testament is supremely a revelation of Jesus Christ. You of course do not find his name until the New Testament, but from Genesis to

Malachi the Scriptures bear witness to him, and apart from him they cannot be adequately understood, or make any proper sense. Jesus said to a group of Jews: 'You diligently study the Scriptures because you think that by them you possess eternal life. These are the Scriptures that testify about me, yet you refuse to come to me to have life.' (John 5:39) He accused them in all their diligent study of the Scriptures, of failing to understand that their end product is a revelation of Jesus himself. To have missed that is to have missed it all. We must read the Old Testament through 'Jesus glasses', interpreting it in the light of he whom it foreshadows and constantly bears witness to. Otherwise it will be little more than a record of Jewish history, or an ancient message to a past era. At best it may be valuable as background to the New Testament, but apart from a few Psalms and choice prophetic statements it will play only a secondary role. On the whole it will be dull!

You will remember that following the crucifixion of Jesus, two disciples were walking the seven miles from Jerusalem to Emmaus. They were disappointed people. Their hopes which had risen and grown for the past three years now lay shattered before them. They said of Jesus 'We had hoped that he was the one who was going to redeem Israel,' (Luke 24:13–32) but their hope was now in the past tense.

In the recent past they had listened to the words of wisdom which had come from his mouth. They had witnessed his mighty power in miraculous acts. They had sat at his feet amazed at the authority with which he spoke, and they had concluded him to be the long-expected Messiah. They shared with all Israel the confident expectations that the Messiah would throw off the shackles of the Roman Empire and restore both their kingdom and their dignity to them once again. Now, those confident expectations lay dashed before them. He was dead. They had not bargained for this. With him in the tomb, the dream had evaporated, the curtain had fallen, the show was over, there was nothing to do but mope.

Then Jesus, risen from the dead, joined them on their walk 'but they were kept from recognizing him.' Having listened patiently to their grief he said to them 'How foolish you are, and how slow of heart to believe all that the prophets have spoken! Did not the Christ have to suffer these things and then enter his glory?' And beginning with Moses and all the Prophets, he explained to them what was said in all the Scriptures concerning himself. What a wonderful Bible study that must have been! If they had captured that on cassette, wouldn't you have wanted to listen to it? What a shame they didn't write it down and reproduce it as a book! This was Jesus exposing Jesus in all the Scriptures. No wonder they said to each other, 'Were not our hearts burning within us while he . . . opened the Scriptures to us?'

Now they had a Bible which made sense. For the first time 'Moses and all the prophets' were alive with meaning and significance. They had found the key which unlocks the treasures of the book and made it all make sense – the Lord Jesus Christ. Have you ever sung the hymn:

> Open my eyes, that I may see,
> Glimpses of truth Thou has for me;
> Place in my hand the wonderful key
> That shall unclasp and set me free.

What is the 'wonderful key' that unclasps the Scriptures and sets us free? It is not a hermeneutic, or a system of theology into which everything must be squeezed. It is Christ himself.

The only adequate exegesis of the Old Testament Scriptures is that which brings us ultimately to Christ, and which does so every time.

Before we are too hard on Jesus' contemporaries we must acknowledge that we have an advantage they did not have. We can read the Bible backwards! We can go back through the New to the Old Testament and interpret it in the subsequent light of the life and ministry of Jesus. This gives us an advantage the Old Testament believers never had.

I don't know if you enjoy Agatha Christie's murder mysteries! When you get to the last chapter, the climax comes when either Hercule Poirot or Miss Marple announce 'whodunit.' I have occasionally guessed correctly who the guilty person is going to be, though not often for the correct reasons! When all the characters in the story (who are lucky enough to still be alive) meet together to hear the verdict, and the plot is revealed, all the clues through the book suddenly seem to have been so obvious. You want to kick yourself for not having picked them up sooner. However, in the unlikely event of reading the book again, you would do so in a very different light. Now you know what is coming, and all the incidental aspects, that previously meant little, flood with intelligent meaning as the book rushes towards its now predictable climax.

Solving The Mystery

I don't want to liken the Bible to an Agatha Christie novel, but I do see something similar in the progression of Scripture. We who have read the final chapter know that from its opening in Genesis, the book is about Jesus. This is how the New Testament writers treat and interpret the Old Testament. The Holy Spirit in inspiring the text planned to reveal the Son of God in the history, rituals and events of the old covenant. At the time the details may seem to have no significance outside of their immediate meaning, but in retrospect the New Testament writers

26

trace the Lord Jesus in the shadows of every page. Speaking of the ceremonial law of the Old Covenant, the writer of Hebrews states: 'The law is only a shadow of the good things that are coming – not the realities themselves.' (Hebrews 10:1) In the New Testament Jesus steps out of the shadows into the sunlight. He is the reality foreshadowed. Looking back from that perspective we recognize his shadow around every corner and in every cul-de-sac of the story.

Paul speaks of the Gospel in its fullness as 'the mystery that has been kept hidden for ages and generations, but is now disclosed to the saints.' (Colossians 1:26) Through the long years of the Old Testament revelation there was always a mystery. Something was always missing. There was always something that did not make sense. The mystery was never solved, but now, declares Paul, the preaching of the Gospel is the declaration of that mystery. It is 'Christ in you, the hope of glory . . . We proclaim him.' (Colossians 1:27–28)

Raiding The Ark

It is with this in mind that we are going to delve into this fascinating aspect of Old Testament symbolism. We may pass through shadows that demand we focus harder than at other times, but we shall discover the living Christ, in the shadows, and find something of what he wants to be in us, and do for us today.

Amongst the many details of the revelation God gave Moses on Mount Sinai, was the instruction for him to build a tabernacle. This was a rectangular tent, forty five feet long and fifteen feet wide, divided into two sections. The Holy Place occupying two-thirds of the space, and the Most Holy Place (sometimes called the Holy of Holies) being the fifteen-feet-square inner chamber. In the Holy Place were three pieces of furniture, a lampstand made of pure gold, a table also overlaid with gold on which was placed the bread of the Presence, and a bronze altar.

Amongst all these utensils, the most important piece of furniture was the ark of the covenant, kept in the Most Holy Place. This was a rectangular box, almost four feet in length, two-and-a-quarter feet in width and the same in height. It was made of acacia wood, overlaid with pure gold both inside and out. On top was placed a golden lid, called in some translations of the Bible the 'mercy seat' and in others 'the atonement cover.' Above this, and forming part of the ark, were two cherubim, made out of hammered gold. They were placed at each end of the ark to face each other, their wings spread upwards to meet in an ark above the atonement cover. The most important thing about the ark, as we have seen, was that God said, 'There . . . I will meet with you.' (Exodus 25:22) God himself often described the ark as 'the place I meet with you.' This was its supreme purpose This was the place where God could meet with man and man could meet with God. This is why the inner chamber of the tabernacle was called the Most Holy Place, for God was there.

In our study we will initially ignore the tabernacle itself, and its various pieces of furniture whose functions were to prepare the way for the High Priest to enter into the Most Holy Place. Instead we are going to go to concentrate on the inner chamber where the High Priest was allowed but once a year on the Day of Atonement. There we find nothing but the ark of the covenant.* It is this we will investigate, and in so doing will discover fundamental

---

*Hebrews 9:4 seems to place the golden altar of incense in the Most Holy Place of the tabernacle, along with the ark of the covenant. In the Old Testament this is always placed in the Holy Place 'in front of the curtain'. Various possible explanations have been given for this seeming designation by the writer of the Hebrews. The most likely is that as he is writing of the activities

truths about the Lord Jesus and his provision for you and me to live the life he created us for.

Cashing The Cheque

Although covered with gold, the ark was stained with blood. On the tenth day of the seventh month of every year the High Priest entered behind the curtain that divided the Most Holy Place from the Holy Place, and in two separate ceremonies he sprinkled the blood of a bull and the blood of a goat to make atonement with God for sin. The blood of the bull atoned for his own sin, and the blood of the goat for the sin of the people. This did not in itself take away sin, it only 'covered sin' because 'it is impossible for the blood of bulls and goats to take away sins.' (Hebrews 10:4) Only the blood of Christ takes away sin.

The blood of bulls and goats functioned like a cheque might function today. The paper on which you write a cheque is worth nothing. The first cheque I ever received in my life was from a school friend. It was made out for one million pounds! In actual fact it was worth nothing for the cheque was only as valid as the cash in the account against which it was written. The account was empty so the cheque was worthless.

Just suppose I want to make a purchase for which I have no cash and the cost of which exceeds the credit that is current in my account. It would be legitimate for me to come to an arrangement whereby I post-date a cheque by a few days to the time I know my account would be able to stand it. In handing over the post-dated cheque, I

---

of the Day of Atonement, the one day in the year when the High Priest drew back the curtain of the Most Holy Place, he is speaking of the altar of incense as being in front of, and alongside, the ark, which, with the curtain opened, it actually was.

receive the goods and treat them as mine. My debt is being 'covered' (though not yet paid for) by the cheque.

The sacrificial system of the Old Testament was the writing of post-dated cheque. It 'covered' sin, in the way my post-dated cheque 'covers' my purchase. The actual money has not yet changed hands. The seller is still out of pocket. The debt is covered but not yet removed. Only when money is in my account can the cheque be cashed and exchanged for the real thing. Then the seller has the money in his pocket. Previously the debt was covered, now it is removed.

The blood of bulls and goats was the cheque, post-dated to Calvary. It acknowledged the debt, it covered the sin, but in itself was of little value. Only at Calvary when the sinless Son of God was made sin, was the debt finally paid. When Jesus Christ cried from the cross 'It is finished', he was declaring that all history might hear 'The debt is paid! The money is in the bank! You can cash your cheque! The sin that for centuries has only been "covered" is now removed. There is no more debt! You are free!'

We no longer post-date the cheque! 'The blood of Jesus, God's Son cleanses us from all sin.' (1 John 1:7) At the moment of true repentance and a willingness to turn from our sin and confess it to Christ, the account of the Lord Jesus is credited to our account in full payment of our sin, and we are free. It is paid in full. Our sin is not only covered, it is removed. We are no longer in debt and can never be called to account for it again. This is the measure of cleansing available through the blood of Jesus.

The ark, the place where God said 'I will meet with you' was always stained with blood, for it is the blood which gives us access to God. It is by the shedding of blood that we have been redeemed, purchased and brought back into fellowship with him. The act of redemption is not in itself the end product of God's purpose. It is the restored relationship with God, for which redemption was a

30

necessary means, that is the end product.

The ark was in the Most Holy Place not that Israel might know forgiveness, but that they might know God. To know God, forgiveness was indispensable, so that having been cleansed of their sin they might approach him with 'clean hands and a pure heart.' (Psalm 24:4) To approach God by any other means was not only unacceptable but dangerous.

At the time the ark had been stolen from Israel by the Philistines, it brought havoc to every town in which they tried to keep it. Eventually, out of despair, they sent it back to Israel on an ox cart pulled by two heifers. As the cart left Philistine territory and approached the border town of Beth Shemesh, the Israelites working in the fields were so excited to see the ark back in their land, they surrounded it, placed the ark on a large rock, chopped up the ox cart to make a fire and offered the cows in sacrifice to God. In their enthusiasm, some of them looked into the ark and tragedy struck. 'God struck down some of the men of Beth Shemesh, putting seventy of them to death because they had looked into the ark of the Lord.' (1 Samuel 6:19) God can only ever be approached on his own terms. Approach God other than on the basis of shed blood as an atonement for sin, and you do not meet him as your friend, you meet him as your judge. We must never play fast and loose with God. We meet with him only in his Son, on the basis of the poured-out blood of Christ on Calvary, the one full and sufficient sacrifice that atones for all time. Approach God in Christ and we are totally safe, fully secure, and we meet him as our Father and as our friend.

To stand before God outside of Christ, I do not meet him as a Father nor as a friend, I meet him only as a judge.

God Lives Amongst People

When we do approach him on his terms, we meet him not

31

only as our friend, but as our very life and source of being.
We discover he has made provision for everything we need
for life and wholeness.

But our concern is not just to approach him, as Aaron
approached the ark of the covenant on the Day of
Atonement to sprinkle the blood. Having made atonement
that reconciles us to him, we want to discover what it is
we find in him that we so desperately need.

In the ark were kept three things: 'the gold jar of manna,
Aaron's staff that had budded, and the stone tablets of
the covenant.' (Hebrews 9:4) We shall discover these to
represent some of the most important ingredients in the
Christian life.

3: Manna: The Gift That Never Satisfied!

The ark of the covenant originally contained only the tablets of stone upon which were written the Ten Commandments. In front of the ark, however, in its position in the Most Holy Place were placed a gold jar of manna and Aaron's staff that had budded. At some stage, these two items were placed in the ark itself along with the tablets of stone, for the book of Hebrews states: 'The ark contained the gold jar of manna, Aarons staff that had budded, and the stone tablets of the covenant.' (Hebrews 9:4) When and why all three were placed in the ark can only be a matter for speculation. When the ark was placed in the holy of holies in Solomon's temple, 'there was nothing in the ark except the two stone tablets that Moses had placed in it at Horeb, where the Lord made a covenant with the Israelites after they came out of Egypt.' (1 Kings 8:9) The very terms of this statement may imply that other things had been there formerly, namely of course, the jar of manna and Aaron's staff, which Hebrews refers to. although the Old Testament itself does not record these as ever being *in* the ark.

If the ark represented the dwelling place of God, then the contents of the ark must represent the meaning of his presence in his people. What is typified in the particular events surrounding the *provision of manna*, the *budding of*

Aaron's staff and the *giving of the law*, reveal central facts regarding the presence of God, the power of God and the purpose of God in the lives of those he indwells today. It is from this perspective we shall look at them together, in the order listed in the book of Hebrews, 'the gold jar of manna, Aaron's staff that had budded and the stone tablets of the covenant'.

The Gold Jar Of Manna

Manna was God's provision of food for Israel during the forty years of their wandering in the wilderness. They had been delivered from Egypt with the purpose of entering into Canaan, 'the land flowing with milk and honey', as quickly as possible. Within six weeks of leaving Egypt they were out of food, they were starting to go round in circles, the novelty of their freedom from slavery was over and 'the whole community grumbled against Moses and Aaron.' What else can people do when they are in trouble, but grumble and look for a scapegoat? 'The Israelites said to them: "If only we had died by the Lord's hand in Egypt! There we sat around pots of meat and ate all the food we wanted, but you have brought us out into this desert to starve this entire assembly to death." ' (Exodus 16:2–3) The result was that God promised them meat in the evening and bread in the morning.

That night quail came and covered the camp, and next morning something remarkable took place. 'In the morning there was a layer of dew around the camp. When the dew was gone, thin flakes like frost on the ground appeared on the desert floor. When the Israelites saw it, they said to each other, "What is it?" for they did not know what it was. Moses said to them, "It is the bread the Lord has given you to eat." ' (Exodus 16:13–15) The instructions then given were very clear. Every morning each person was to gather as much as he needed for that day. 'No one is to keep any of it until morning.' (Exodus 16:19) On the sixth day they were to gather enough for the seventh as on that day there would be no fresh provision.

The Lord Jesus Christ very clearly identified this provision of manna with himself. Speaking with a group of Jews they said to him, 'Our forefathers ate the manna in the desert; as it is written: "He gave them bread to eat." Jesus said to them, "I tell you the truth, it is not Moses who has given you the bread from heaven, but it is my Father who gives you the true bread from heaven. For the bread of God is he who comes down from heaven and gives life to the world . . . I am the bread of life." ' (John 6:31–35) There are many lessons to be learned from the provision of manna representing in some way the Lord Jesus Christ. Only one, I suggest, depicts the true message God was teaching Israel, but there are a number of incidental truths that can be seen.

Although by no means the main point of the story, one incidental aspect is worth commenting on.

Yesterday's Supply Is Inadequate For Today

Being told to gather only enough for each day, predictably there were those amongst the people who paid no attention to these details and kept part of the first morning's provision for the second day. On that morning, they rolled over in bed, glad to be able to stay a little longer than their neighbours who were out early, busily gathering the fresh supply of manna for the day. When they eventually rose to eat yesterday's stored manna for today's breakfast, they found 'it was full of maggots and began to smell.' (Exodus 16:20) That may well have added to its protein content, but not to its attractiveness!

It is very possible to be drawing on provisions of God that have grown maggot-ridden and smelly! He gave to us yesterday what met our needs yesterday. But this is today, and 'His compassions never fail, they are new every morning, great is your faithfulness,' wrote Jeremiah. (Lamentations 3:22–23) God is fresh every morning, and the moment I start to draw on yesterday's provisions for today's needs my experience is in danger of growing stale. What God did for me yesterday may have been fresh, wonderful and adequate, but this is today and he has new plans and new resources for today.

In my teenage years, having recently become a Christian, I went with a group of young people from my area to Capernwray Hall (where I now live), a young people's Christian holiday centre (and Bible School) in the North of England. We went for a week in the summer, geared especially for teenagers. It was a great time and I heard things about the Christian life I had never heard before, or if I had, they had not registered with me. At the end of the week I went home excited by everything I had learned, by the atmosphere I had been part of, and the people who had made an impact on me. Drawing on these great experiences I found that my excitement lasted only for about a week, and I slid back into the old dull routine again.

The following year I went back to Capernwray for two weeks, and caught again the previous year's enthusiasm. Before leaving at the end of that time, I remember telling one of the leaders that although last year had been a good year, it had fallen flat when I returned home. However, I assured him that I intended this year to be different! I set off home full of enthusiasm and excitement. I managed to keep the momentum going for about ten days, only to find myself back in the old rut again.

As a solution to the problem I began to say to myself 'I must go to Capernwray Hall more often,' and found ways of going twice a year until I began spending some of my school holidays enrolled on the temporary summer

36

staff. In between times I attended one or two young people's weekend conferences that would keep me 'topped up', while looking around for other places where I could put my spiritual batteries on charge for a while. I could then live off my filled batteries until they were exhausted again and needed to go back for another recharge! This was the kind of mentality I had for several years.

Then I made a simple discovery! The source of blessing was not Capernwray or conferences, it was Jesus Christ. He did not live at Capernwray Hall, or hide away in conference centres, or come out for special meetings, but Jesus Christ lived in me, and his mercies, his supplies, his compassions, his strength, his wisdom and his riches were 'new every morning'. As a child of God I had the privilege of being able to wake up to every new day and say with confidence, 'Thank you Lord Jesus for the new, fresh supply of resources you have for me today. Thank you for whatever you did for me and gave to me yesterday. But this is a new day, and yesterday's supplies are not necessary nor adequate for today. You have something fresh and new for the present.' What a joy to go into every new day and every new responsibility and every new opportunity with the confidence that all I ever need for the present moment is available right now in Jesus Christ. 'His divine power has given us everything we need for life and godliness through our knowledge of him.' (2 Peter 1:3)

Recently, at the end of a meeting at which I had been speaking, a man came to talk to me. He told me that fifteen years ago, in his late teens, he had known, loved and experienced God in a very real way. When he reached twenty he began to drift, got involved in some things that were not good and before long was right away from God, with hardly any thought or concern about him. Six months before the time we met, his cousin had been killed in a road accident, and at the funeral service he had been challenged to come back to God and to get right with him.

This he had done, and for six months he had given his life over to Christ, got involved in a good church, and begun to read his Bible again. 'But', he explained to me, 'when I was in my late teens I had such an awareness of God in my life that I haven't been able to recapture. He was real, I knew he loved me and I knew that I loved him. Since coming back to God I have been trying to get that experience and feeling back. I ask God all the time to give me back what I had then, and he doesn't seem to be doing so.' I asked him if it had ever occurred to him that God perhaps wasn't really interested in giving him back what he had fifteen years ago. God has moved on. He is not the God of fifteen years ago, he is the God of today. I suggested he stopped asking God to repeat the experience of fifteen years ago and instead to affirm before God every morning. 'Thank you Lord Jesus for what you have for me today. What you did fifteen years ago was great, but you are alive today and you have plans for me today and provisions for me today and I want you to do in me today what you have planned for me today.'

This is why the Christian life is so fresh and up-to-date! We are not living in a past experience, or on stale encounters, valuable and wonderful as they were and the memory of them still is, but we have a God who is fresh and new! His name is Jehovah, meaning 'I am', not 'I was', the One who operates eternally in the present tense.

God gave the manna as a fresh provision every morning that would meet their need for that day. The next day's supply would be available tomorrow. They would not need it today.

That I am sure is a good and wonderful thing to know, but I suggest that is not really the point of the manna!

Godly But Deadly

There is a very interesting twist to this provision of manna.

Although the Lord Jesus identified it with himself, it did not satisfy the people. It was the biggest source of their dissatisfaction and grumbling during the forty years of their wandering. 'The rabble with them began to crave other food, and again the Israelites started wailing and said, "If only we had meat to eat! We remember the fish we ate in Egypt at no cost – also the cucumbers, melons, leeks, onions and garlic. But now we have lost our appetite; we never see anything but this manna." ' (Numbers 11:4–5) Then is described the lengths to which they tried to go to give it some variety. They probably ate it fresh for breakfast – 'they ground it in a handmill or crushed it in a mortar. They cooked it in a pot or made it into cakes.' One day they might fry it, another day roast it or toast it. They might make manna pie or mannaburgers, put ketchup on it or custard, but however they tried to spice it up or disguise it, it was the same old manna, morning, noon and night and they grew sick of it!

Not only was it tedious as a diet, but its most fundamental problem was that however they cooked or prepared it, it actually never satisfied them. 'He humbled you, causing you to hunger and then feeding you with manna.' (Deuteronomy 8:3) What kind of food is that? In eating it they were humbled and caused to hunger, fed again with manna, and soon hungry yet again! Here is a provision from God that did not satisfy them. Why on earth did God command Moses to 'Take an omer of manna and keep it for the generations to come, so that they can see the bread I gave you to eat in the desert when I brought you out of Egypt.' (Exodus 16:32) Surely the sooner they forgot about it the better! Even God could be embarrassed about it as a provision of food. Perhaps to remember how bad it was they might keep a little in a museum somewhere! But keep it in front of the ark of the covenant, the place God met with his people in the Most Holy Place, and then in the ark itself? This is almost preposterous!

There must be something very important here, and I suggest that there is. I am sure you have discovered that the best commentary on the Bible is always the Bible itself! It also happens to be the most reliable! In the light of other parts of Scripture there are two very interesting descriptions of manna that give us important clues as to its timeless meaning. Firstly, 'it was white like coriander seed and tasted like wafers made with honey.' (Exodus 16:31) There is a vital clue: 'it tasted of *honey*.' Where was God taking them at this time? You will remember that when God called Moses at the burning bush he promised about Israel, 'I have come down to rescue them from the hand of the Egyptians and to bring them up out of that land into a good and spacious land, a land *flowing with milk and honey*.' (Exodus 3:8) This was somewhere they were supposed to enter within a matter of days or at most weeks.

Deuteronomy 1.2 states: 'It takes eleven days to go from Horeb to Kadesh Barnea by the Mount Sier road.' Kadesh Barnea was more than half way, though it took them two years to reach there, then another thirty-eight years to reach Canaan. In fact, the Bible records: 'When the Lord sent you out from Kadesh Barnea he said, "Go up and take possession of the land I have given you." But you rebelled against the command of the Lord your God. You did not trust him or obey him.' (Deuteronomy 9:23) At Kadesh Barnea the land of Canaan was in their reach and God intended them to take it there and then! Instead they wandered for another thirty eight years in disobedience. A total of forty years for a journey designed to last not more than two or three weeks!

Recently I had occasion to travel the same journey. I had been fulfilling speaking engagements in Egypt immediately followed by an engagement in Jerusalem. With my brother-in-law, I took a bus that left Cairo at

7 am and arrived in Jerusalem at 5 pm; and that included about a four hour stop at the border. In total the journey was no more than six hours of actual travelling, on roads that for most of the time were not conducive to high speeds! The distance is less than three hundred miles. It is true that God did not take Israel by the most direct route, which would have been through hostile Philistine territory; nevertheless I work out their average speed, as the crow flies, to have been around thirty-six yards per day. By any standards, that is not fast!

The purpose God had in mind for them was not just to set them free from Egypt. Crossing the Red Sea to liberty was not the object of the exercise. Though in itself a wonderful moment they would commemmorate every year in the Passover celebrations that continue until today, it was only the means to an end. His purpose in bringing them out from Egypt was to bring them *into* Canaan. 'He *brought you out* of Egypt by his presence and his great strength . . . to *bring you in* to their land to give it to you for your inheritance.' (Deuteronomy 4:37-38) The purpose of their being brought *out*, was that they might be brought *in*. 'I am the Lord your God who brought you out of Egypt to give you the land of Canaan and to be your God.' (Leviticus 25:38)

Now the people were out of Egypt, but they were not yet in Canaan, the land flowing with milk and honey which was their ultimate destination. In the meantime, God did not intend to satisfy them in the wilderness, so he gave them food to eat which 'tasted of honey', that is, it tasted of the real thing, but was not the real thing. Before we explore the meaning of that, let me point out something else which is not so explicitly stated but which I find interesting. It says of the manna that 'it was white', (Exodus 16:31) and appeared as 'a layer of dew around the camp.' (Exodus 16:31) As it dried, 'thin flakes like frost appeared on the desert floor.' Its initial appearance was as something 'white' and 'wet'. Only later did it dry and look like frost. As the dawn broke each new day and the Israelites scanned the ground to see if God had provided fresh manna yet again, its appearance would almost certainly remind them of milk. If that is so we may say that the manna looked like the real thing, *milk*, and it tasted like the real thing, *honey*, but it was not the real thing. It had no real body or substance to it, for it was 'thin flakes . . . like wafers.' (Exodus 16:14,31) Not the normal ingredients of a good and satisfying meal! Would you like to eat thin wafers three times a day? You certainly would not get fat on that!

There is another description of the manna which is slightly different, but similar in significance. 'It tasted like something made with *olive oil*.' (Numbers 11:8) Right through Scripture oil is a consistent symbol of the Holy Spirit. As an example, when David was anointed as King by Samuel, 'Samuel took the horn of oil and anointed him in the presence of his brothers, and from that day on the Spirit of the Lord came upon David in power.' (1 Samuel 16:13) The anointing with oil portrayed the coming of the Holy Spirit on David to equip him for the new function God had given to him as king of Israel.

The fresh provision of manna every morning, which in its white appearance and taste of honey reminded them of the real thing – the land flowing with milk and honey, at the same time in its 'taste of honey' revealed to them the Holy Spirit's presence as the one who sustains. It was the witness of the continual presence of the Holy Spirit amongst them, through all these long years, and in spite of their continual disobedience. Years later Nehemiah records: 'You gave your good Spirit to instruct them. You did not withhold your manna from their mouths, and you gave them water for their thirst. For forty years you sustained them in the desert.' (Nehemiah 9:20–21) But to sustain is not to satisfy, and although the manna

42

contained all the ingredients of God's full provision for his people, it did not satisfy them, and left them grumbling, looking over their shoulders and wishing for an opportunity to go back to Egypt.

Tragic as this may be, it is a very accurate picture of so many Christian people. If you were to ask them if they have come to the cross and received the forgiveness of their sins through the shed blood of Jesus Christ, they would tell you they have. If you asked them if they had been born again of the Spirit of God, they would confidently assert it was true. If you asked them if Christ now lived in them and that their bodies were temples of his Spirit, they would tell you that they believe it. But if you then asked them if they were satisfied, they would hang their heads in embarrassment. They are not satisfied, they are bored, they are frustrated, they are empty, and when no one else is around they are looking over their shoulders at the Egypt they have left behind, wondering if they should go back, even wishing that they could.

Sealed But Not Filled

If this is true of you, let me explain what is happening to you. The moment you came to God in repentance and faith, your sin was forgiven, you did receive the Holy Spirit whose presence in you is the gift of eternal life. Paul affirmed to the Ephesian Christians: 'And you also were included in Christ when you heard the word of truth, the gospel of your salvation. Having believed, you were marked in him with a seal, the promised Holy Spirit, who is a deposit guaranteeing our inheritance until the redemption of those who are God's possession.' (Ephesians 1:13–14) This is true of every genuinely born again believer in the Lord Jesus Christ. They have been 'sealed' for ever, by the Holy Spirit whose presence in them makes them a true Christian.

But to be indwelt by the Spirit of Christ is not the end

43

of the story, it is the 'guarantee of an inheritance' that is to be entered into. It is therefore the beginning of a process of discovery and growth. Paul goes on to say to the Ephesians: 'I keep asking that the God of our Lord Jesus Christ, the glorious Father may give you the Spirit of wisdom and revelation, so that you may know him better.' (Ephesians 1:17) Knowing Christ has its beginning in the Holy Spirit's revelation to us of who he is and why we need him, but from that initial encounter must come a continuing process of revelation that deepens and broadens. Paul then writes to the same people: 'I pray that out of his glorious riches, he may strengthen you with power through his Spirit in your inner being.' (Ephesians 3:16) The Holy Spirit's role has to do with strengthening us with power, increasingly to be discovered and drawn upon. This is not an experience in history, but a continual appropriation that grows and deepens. Then, to the same people who have been sealed by the Spirit, for whom he prays an increasing revelation of Christ by the Spirit and greater strengthening with power by the Spirit, he commands them 'Be filled with the Spirit'. (Ephesians 5:18) Rejoicing as he does in the salvation of the Ephesian Christians, Paul is telling them that this is not enough . . . there is more, and more. Not of substance for he has also told them 'God . . . has blessed us in the heavenly realms with every spiritual blessing in Christ.' (Ephesians 1:3) Apart from Christ God has nothing to give for there is nothing more, but I may have his presence whilst knowing little of his power! I may be sealed by his Spirit but not filled by his Spirit.

Brought Out To Be Brought In

God's purpose for Israel was not to get them out of Egypt. That was only a necessary means to an end. His purpose was to take them into Canaan. His purpose for you is not to get you out of the guilt and consequences of your sin, wonderful as that would be even if it was the end product of your salvation. But there is more! His purpose is to get you into that condition where the Holy Spirit can begin to reproduce the character of Jesus Christ in you. In the wilderness God sustained Israel with the manna but he never satisfied Israel with the manna, for they were to be satisfied only in Canaan. God will sustain you with the presence of his Spirit, for our security is guaranteed in him, but he will never satisfy you outside of his fullness. We have been brought out of our sin, not so that we might reach heaven by the skin of our teeth, but that we might 'be filled to the measure of all the fullness of God'. (Ephesians 3:19) Then, ruling as our Lord and filling with his Spirit, he might build into us the character of Jesus and do through us the work of Jesus.

Unless you or I are prepared to go all the way with God, and live in complete surrender to his authority, in obedience to his will and in the fullness of his Spirit, one thing is clear, we will never be satisfied with Christ. We will be dissatisfied and uncomfortable. This is why the Holy Spirit may be a very uncomfortable person in your life. If, at your invitation, he is in you, you cannot go back for you are 'sealed for the day of redemption'. Instead you may grieve and quench the Holy Spirit and do your best to subdue him, but every day there will be the taste of honey on your lips, the taste of oil in your heart, as the Holy Spirit bears witness that you are a child of God, and you will be deeply dissatisfied. As a direct result, one of two things will begin to happen. Either out of disappointment and frustration you will begin to long for his fullness, or you will begin to hate his presence in your life and do all to resist him.

Two people I know well have illustrated this to me. One, a man who came to know Christ in his twenties and after a year or two returned to his old life. He tells of how back in the old routine, with the old habits, the old sins and the old acquaintances there was one marked difference to his earlier experience. Before he had become a Christian he had enjoyed everything he did. Now, doing identical things with the same people, he no longer did or could enjoy them. Every morning he rose, and every night as he went to his bed, the taste of honey and oil in his heart bore witness that he was a child of God and could therefore never be satisfied outside of Christ. This nagging role of the Holy Spirit became for him the evidence that he was a genuine Christian, and in consequence he came back to Christ, and to a life of fulfilment and satisfaction. Another I know, became a true Christian and was enthusiastic and committed. He gave his time to serving God and took a number of months out to engage in short term missionary service. A while later he went away from God, and has been away now for several of years. The interesting thing is that although he would tell you he has satisfied himself that Christianity is not true and there are other more valid explanations for life, he spends much of his time attacking and undermining the Gospel, even going to the lengths of writing a doctoral thesis attacking the reality of Christian experience. Why? Because every morning, the taste of honey and oil, the witness of the Holy Spirit, is alive in his heart, and he must do all he can to drown and crush that witness. He never will of course, and so rather than come back to God as my first friend did, he resists him.

The presence of the manna on the ground every morning was a symbol of the fact that God will never, never let his people go. He has made a covenant, and he will not break it. 'If we are faithless, he will remain faithful, for he cannot disown himself.' (2 Timothy 2:13) If any people had given God reason to leave them, Israel had! They were hardly across the Red Sea than they were hankering to return to their slavery. They complained, they rebelled, they engaged in idolatory and every kind of sin you could imagine. There must have been times Moses despaired of God ever staying with them. Surely he would leave them now! Yet at first

46

light of every dawn, he would scan the ground and there would be the fresh manna, yet again. God had not forsaken them! Though they had long forsaken him, he still provided the witness to himself. It was the seal of his covenant with them, the taste of honey, the taste of oil, and he would never let them go. I do not know who is reading these pages, but I do know this. If God has begun a work in your life, you can be sure he will not rest in his purpose to bring it to completion. But he will not force the issue. He will not twist your arm nor put a pistol to your head. You can choose if you wish to die in the desert, as most of Israel did, but you will do so resisting the witness of his Spirit in your heart, every morning of every new day.

Only One Solution

There was only one solution for boring manna! It was not that someone compile a new recipe book to spice up the old dull routine. The solution was very simple. Get into Canaan! Having crossed the Jordan River, the Israelites celebrated the Passover: 'The day after the Passover, that very day, they ate some of the produce of the land: unleavened bread and roasted grain. The manna stopped the day after they ate this food from the land; there was no longer any manna for the Israelites, but that year they ate of the produce of Canaan.' (Joshua 5:11–12) Now they feasted on the rich provision God had always intended for them, and it was the only solution to their dissatisfaction. Why didn't Israel enter the land sooner? Why did they have to loose a whole generation? Apart from two men, no one who was over twenty when they left Egypt, ever arrived in Canaan. A whole generation died in the wilderness. Why are so many Christians dissatisfied, living in spiritual poverty and not entering in to all God has planned for them? The answers to these two questions are similar, and we will explore them in the next chapter.

47

4: Refusing To Believe

The fall-out rate in many churches is high. I know one rural church that in twenty years always had a youth work and programme for young people. Most of these young people in the course of time made a 'profession of faith' in Christ yet, as far as I know, not one ever matured into a vibrant, healthy, holy Christian, sold out to Jesus Christ and a useful member of his body. Another leader told me 'before our young people reach eighteen, we have lost most of them.' He then went on to ask if in the course of my travels I had come across any good ideas or good programmes for keeping young people interested. I understand his question, but it is not programmes, or activities or even leaders that keep young people. These are all important and require careful thought and planning. But to discuss keeping young people on that basis is like discussing various new ways of cooking and serving manna! The manna is dull, repetitive and monotonous. In itself it does not and will not satisfy. We try at least to prolong the agony of that discovery by making it as attractive as we possibly can in the meantime. You will remember there is only one lasting solution to boring manna, and that is to get into Canaan where 'there is no longer any manna for the Israelites, but instead they ate of the produce of Canaan.' (Joshua 5:12) The only solution to boring Christianity is that full blooded relationship with God that Jesus died and rose again to make possible. Only

48

then are we satisfied. Only then is it exciting. Only then do things happen.

We asked the question at the conclusion of the last chapter, Why did Israel not enter Canaan sooner? In the answer to that question we shall consider a reason why so many Christians do not enter into the fullness that God has planned for them in his Son, the Lord Jesus Christ.

Fear Of The Enemy

There are two basic reasons. The first was fear. The book of Numbers reports: 'The Lord said to Moses, "Send some men to explore the land of Canaan, which I am giving to the Israelites. From each ancestral tribe send one of its leaders." ' So twelve leaders, one from each tribe, were sent with instructions to examine every part of the land. They were to go to the hill country, down the valleys, and through the desert. They were to check the towns, the soil, the vegetation and bring back samples of its fruit. They set out, and forty days later returned, mission accomplished. 'They came back to Moses and Aaron and the whole Israelite community . . . They gave Moses this account: "We went into the land to which you sent us, and it does flow with milk and honey! Here is its fruit." '
In other words, they were saying that Moses was absolutely right, and God was absolutely right. The land was rich. It did flow with milk and honey, and to confirm it, they brought back some pomegranates, figs and a single cluster of grapes that took two men to carry on a pole between them.

God's promises were true and unexaggerated. 'But . . .' they said, 'we are sorry to disappoint you that there is bad news too . . . the people who live there are powerful, and the cities are fortified and very large. We even saw descendants of Anak there. The Amalakites live in the Negev; the Hittites, Jebusites and Amorites live in the hill country; and the Canaanites live near the sea and along the Jordan . . . We can't attack these people, they are stronger than we are . . . The land we explored devours those living in it.' (Numbers 13:1; 26–33) The land may be flowing with milk and honey, but it is flowing with enemies, opposition, and inevitable warfare too. And they were absolutely right. Taking into account this likely force of opposition, their solution was simple: 'They said to each other, "We should choose a leader and go back to Egypt." ' (Numbers 14:4) Of the twelve spies, two held a different opinion, Joshua and Caleb. 'Then Caleb silenced the people before Moses and said, "We should go up and take possession of the land, for we can certainly do it." ' (Numbers 13:30) This was not some maverick attempt to take on the challenge, win or die. This was an unshatterable confidence that God who promised them Canaan would deliver Canaan. The promise, to Caleb and Joshua, was as good as the fulfilment, for the promise was as certain in prospect as the fulfilment would be in retrospect. 'If the Lord is pleased with us, he will lead us into that land, a land flowing with milk and honey, and will give it to us. Their protection is gone, but the Lord is with us. Do not be afraid of them.' (Numbers 14:8–9)

The root of the response of the ten was fear. Fear that was derived from a sense of hopelessness when faced with opposition, bigger and stronger than their ability to cope.

Feast And Fight

Victory and ease should never be confused or made synonymous. To say that God gives victory does not mean we do not fight. To be called to fight does not mean the victory is in doubt or dependent upon our ability. The victory is God's, the battle is ours. I love the combination of these two aspects in the best known Psalm and possibly best loved passage in all of Scripture, Psalm 23. 'You

50

prepare a table before me in the presence of my enemies.' (Psalm 23:5) There are two things in that statement. A *feast* and a *fight*. 'You prepare a table before me', that is the feast, representing the full provision of everything we need. We do not earn it, we do not prepare it and we do not fight for it. It is prepared and provided by God and given to us freely. But where is the feast? The startling answer is 'in the presence of my enemies'. It is in the thick of a battle, nose to nose, eyeball to eyeball with the enemy. If we are to enjoy the feast we must engage in the fight. If we avoid the fight we avoid the feast. Everything the ten spies said about Canaan was true. Every conclusion they drew about the size and might of the occupying people was correct. At no time is it ever right to undermine the strength of the enemy or the ferocity of the battle, but we must never look at that and fail to take into account the victory of the Lord Jesus Christ. 'For our struggle is not against flesh and blood, but against the rulers, against the authorities, against the powers of this dark world and against the spiritual forces of evil in the heavenly realms. Therefore put on the full armour of God . . .' (Ephesians 6:12–13) The battle is real and the enemies are known.

There was a time when I thought that the more one grew in the Christian life, the easier it became. Temptations would ease, the old nature would lie down and the devil would give up! Now I have learned there are no grounds for that assumption at all. The reverse is more likely to be true. The more we grow in Christ, the more we unsettle the devil and the hotter becomes the battle.

I will not forget going with my wife to visit Dr Alan Redpath shortly before he died in 1989. He was well known throughout the Christian world for a ministry that enriched thousands of people. He had suffered two strokes which left him paralysed down one side and confined to a wheelchair in his hospital room. During our visit he told us he had never known an intensity of spiritual warfare

51

such as he was experiencing in that condition. 'You would have thought the devil would have given up on an old man like me,' he said. I reminded him that perhaps the devil had a few old scores to settle. After decades of powerful ministry all around the world, here was a man, not retreating from the battle, but more conscious of its intensity than ever before, and still giving Satan trouble. But I will tell you something else about Alan Redpath. Few enjoyed the *feast as he did, but perhaps few experience the fight as he did too.*

Defeat of The Last Enemy

Paul who warns about the reality of the battle and the need for being armed, also tells us of Christ, 'He must reign until he has put all his enemies under his feet. The last enemy to be destroyed is death. For he has put everything under his feet.' (1 Corinthians 15:25–27) In the context of that statement, Paul is writing of the resurrection of Jesus from the dead, in which he defeated 'the last enemy', and having defeated the last enemy he has defeated every other enemy. This is accomplished fact. But the battle is still on, the enemy 'prowls around like a roaring lion looking for someone to devour', (1 Peter 5:8) for he is still at large and will fight to the end, though he is beaten and he knows it!

It is usually the enemy who believes more confidently in the victory over him than the people of God do. When Joshua had succeeded Moses as leader of Israel, he sent two spies to look over Jericho. The nation was shortly to cross the Jordan River, and having done so, their first obstacle would be the walled city of Jericho. The spies made friends with a prostitute named Rahab. In exchange for the promise to spare her life when Israel came eventually to take the city, she hid them in her house on the city wall. Before the spies lay down to sleep on the first night, she came to talk with them and said, 'I know the Lord has given this land to you and that a great fear of you has fallen on us, so that all who live in this country are melting in fear because of you. We have heard how the Lord dried up the water of the Red Sea for you when you came out of Egypt, and what you did to Sihon and Og the two kings of the Amorites east of the Jordan, whom you completely destroyed. When we heard of it our hearts melted and everyone's courage failed because of you, for the Lord your God is God in heaven above and on the earth below.' (Joshua 2:9–11) This is a representative of the enemy speaking! It has been forty years since God dried up the Red Sea, and for those forty years the inhabitants of Jericho have had their watchmen scanning the horizon for any sign of a crowd of people heading their way. And they knew that when Israel eventually came, Jericho's days were numbered. By their own reckoning, they did not stand a chance, for 'the Lord has given this land to you.' The victory was already the Israelites.

Meanwhile, the Israelites themselves had been wandering in the desert, scared of any advance into enemy territory. Even the spies sent to investigate Jericho were cowering on the roof of the house where Rahab had hidden them. After she had told them of Jericho's confidence that God would give their land to Israel and having begged them to show kindness to her when that day eventually came, they assured her 'We will treat you kindly and faithfully when the Lord gives us the land.' (Joshua 2:14) Notice an important difference between the certainty of Rahab and the understanding of the spies. Rahab had said, 'The Lord has given you the land.' To her it was past tense, already determined and only awaiting its execution. The land was Israel's. It was given them by God. The spies had responded that they would take care of her 'when the Lord gives us the land'. To them it was still future tense, yet to be determined, but like chickens, not to be counted

53

before hatched. It was their earnest prayer that this might one day be so, but it was unwise to presume!

Isn't that amazing? Every day that Jericho waited for the news that Israel was on its way and that their own days were numbered, the Israelites were living in fear of the enemy they might one day have to encounter! But that seems so typical, even now. The one who believes most strongly in the victory of Jesus Christ is the enemy! 'You believe that there is one God. Good! Even the demons believe that – and shudder.' (James 2:19)

This is a remarkable picture. Do not think of the devil and his demons as confident and cocky. The medieval picture of Satan as dressed in a skin tight suit looking like an overgrown cat with pitchfork, tail and horns has no resemblance to the truth. I like to think of the devil as someone cowering in the corner, his hair standing on end, trembling with fright! This is a New Testament picture of a condemned, defeated foe. The devil needs no convincing that Jesus Christ is King of kings and Lord of lords, and has defeated sin, the world and the devil. It is only Christians who need convincing of that! What may be a future hope as far as our belief is concerned is history as far as God is concerned. He only waits for us to allow him to implement what has already been obtained and made possible, 'Thanks be to God. He gives us the victory through our Lord Jesus Christ.' (1 Corinthians 15:57)

The Way Out And The Way In

There is a simple principle behind all of this that Israel had failed to reckon on. The God who brought Israel out of Egypt was the same God who would bring Israel in to Canaan. It was not a case of God getting them out of Egypt, but now they must employ all their resourcefulness, strength and wisdom to get themselves into Canaan.

Not only was it the same God. The means by which he delivered them from Egypt were the same means by which he would deliver them to Canaan. He opened the Red Sea to bring them *out*. He would open the Jordan River to bring them *in*. They had trusted God to intervene when they stood on the banks of the Red Sea, unable to cross and unable to defend themselves against the Egyptian forces. Pharaoh had changed his mind about their release and was coming from behind to round them up and take them back as slaves once again. There the people had cried out to Moses. There Moses had cried out to God. Then Moses had turned in absolute confidence to the people and declared: 'The Lord will fight for you; you need only be still.' (Exodus 14:14) True to his word, God did fight for them. It was miraculous and dramatic. A strong east wind blew through the night and when the dawn broke in the eastern sky the Israelites awoke to discover a divide in the sea and they walked to freedom on dry ground.

The Israelites were in no doubt as to who was responsible. It was not Moses but God. Immediately on the other side they broke into song, and for eighteen verses told of the great thing God had done. 'I will sing to the Lord . . . he is highly exalted . . . The Lord is my strength and my song, he has become my salvation. He is my God . . . The Lord is a warrior . . . Your right hand, O Lord, was majestic in power. Your right hand, O Lord, shattered the enemy . . . The Lord will reign for ever and ever.' (Exodus 15:1–18) In all their celebration and praise there was not a word about Moses! There was no carrying him on their shoulders and singing 'For he's a jolly good fellow.' Moses was not even mentioned, for the people knew and Moses knew that it was not Moses who had delivered them, but God.

If you are a Christian, someone may be responsible for having led you to Christ. You will be forever grateful to that person, but lead you to Christ is all they did. It is

55

Christ alone who saved you, and it is he exclusively who is to be praised. If God uses you to bring others to Christ then rejoice that that is so, but do not take it too personally. Do not credit yourself with their salvation. Do not regard them as your convert.

If the way out of Egypt was by divine intervention, where only God could be credited with having done it, so the way in to Canaan was to be by divine intervention where only God could be credited with doing it. Moses was dead. Joshua was the new leader. God told him: 'I am with you as I was with Moses.' (Joshua 3:7) Joshua prepared the people by declaring, 'Consecrate yourselves, for tomorrow the Lord will do amazing things among you . . . This is how you will know that the living God is among you.' (Joshua 3:5,10) This is not something for which Joshua will be responsible. God is going to intervene. God is going to do something – God *has* to do something. The ark of the covenant, was to be carried in to the Jordan River on the shoulders of the priests. It just so happened that the river was in flood, yet the moment the feet of the priests carrying the ark touched the waters edge the stream stopped flowing. They stood on the dry ground of the river bed and the whole nation passed by coming up on to the side of Canaan. When the priests carrying the ark then came up from the river it began to flow normally and returned to its flood stage as before. Joshua explained to the people 'The Lord your God did to the Jordan just what he had done to the Red Sea when he dried it up before us until we had crossed over. He did this so that all the peoples of the earth might know that the hand of the Lord is powerful and so that you might always fear the Lord your God.' (Joshua 5:23–24)

In other words, God is letting you know that the way you came out of Egypt is the way you come into Canaan. The way you begin to walk with God is the way you continue to walk with God. You did not let God bring you out so that you might bring yourselves in; rather the One who brought you out is the only One who can bring you in.

This is so wonderfully true of the Christian life. 'So then, just as you received Christ Jesus as Lord, continue to live in him.' (Colossians 2:6) The Authorized Version states: 'As ye have therefore received Christ Jesus the Lord, so walk ye in him.' *As* you did one thing, receive him, so do the other, walk in him. The way you live in him is the way you received him! You received him on the basis of repentance and faith. By repentance you turned from all that you are, and by faith you embraced all that he is. You recognized your sin which is a consequence of your inability to live by your own resources, and you recognized that only Christ could transform you. This is exactly what it takes to live in the fullness and power of God's Spirit. You turn from everything you are, placing 'no confidence in the flesh' (Philippians 3:3) and embrace everything that he is, acknowledging it is in his strength alone that you live. You exchange your sin for his righteousness, your weakness for His strength and your poverty for his riches. This is the Christian life. Ultimately it is the exchange of your life for his. As he once saved you from the guilt of your sin, so he now saves you from the power of your sin, not on the basis of what you do for him, but on the basis of what you let him do in you.

Israel did not enter Canaan sooner because of fear! The enemy was there, but so were the resources available to them in God. They were more aware of the strength of the enemy than of the power of God. Consequently, the only logical response was to be afraid. If you do not know what the Lord Jesus Christ has accomplished for you, not only in deliverance from your guilt, but also in the provision of all that it takes for you to be godly and effective in this life, then you will know this fear. We face real enemies in the world, the flesh and the devil. You will have no grounds for confidence should you take them on yourself, no matter how sincerely or enthusiastically. You will retreat with your tail between your legs again and again and begin to lose hope of it ever being different.

We will explore later exactly what it is about the work of Jesus that sets us free. In the meantime, begin to believe that he has the victory!

Refusing To Believe

There is a second reason why Israel did not enter the land sooner. When the spies returned from Canaan and ten of them declared it an impossible task, God asked the question: 'How long will they refuse to believe in me, in spite of all the miraculous signs I have performed among them?' (Numbers 14:11) Their problem was one of refusing to believe. It was not so much an intellectual problem as a volitional one. God had repeatedly revealed himself to them and demonstrated his power on their behalf. They had no rational excuses for denying God's ability, nor doubting his promises. They actually refused to believe! They did not want to know what God could do.

Sadly, there are some people who seem content to stay exactly where they are. They do not want to know that things could be different. Although they are Christians, as Israel was God's people, they resist the message of the sufficiency of Christ and his desire to do better things for them and with them. Like Israel, afraid of the battle, they have learned to be content with the wilderness.

God can do nothing with the person who refuses to believe. He does not frog-march us into Canaan. Of the six hundred thousand men over the age of twenty who left Egypt, only two entered Canaan forty years later. They were the only two who believed. That belief was not an intellectual assent to God's person, or to his purpose or his power. No doubt the creed of most of the Israelites who did not enter Canaan was correct and fully orthodox, but something more than that was needed. The belief that acknowledges what God can do and lets him do it! The belief which looks beyond what *God says* to what *God is*. It does not consider the credibility of what God has said but the invincibility of who God is. When God finds people who will listen carefully to what he has said, who will believe fully in what he has promised, and then confidently allow him to do it, things start to happen. 'The one who calls you is faithful and he will do it ' (1 Thessalonians 5:24) It was God who called them to Canaan. It was God who got them there. It is God who has called you to live a holy life, it is God who will make it possible. Do you believe him? Will you trust him?

5: Aaron's Staff That Budded

We have seen that the gold jar of manna, placed in the ark of the covenant, represents the presence of God with his people. Having been born again of the Holy Spirit, we have been sealed by the Holy Spirit. We may refuse to go all the way with God, and choose to live in the barren wilderness instead of enjoying the riches of Canaan, nevertheless there will be that witness of the Holy Spirit in our hearts that we are children of God. We will either be drawn to know him more deeply, or driven to resist him more definitely. But lose him we will not, for God is utterly faithful, even in the face of our unfaithfulness.

Along with the manna, the ark contained 'Aaron's staff that had budded.' (Hebrews 9:4) If manna speaks of the *presence of God* in the life of every true believer, Aaron's staff speaks of the *power of God* that is to be evident in every true believer.

To discover what this is all about, we have to go to a story in Numbers, chapters sixteen and seventeen. There was an uprising taking place against Moses and Aaron. It involved two hundred and fifty influential men, 'well-known community leaders who had been appointed members of the council'. These men came as a group to oppose Moses and Aaron, and their complaint was 'You have gone too far! The whole community is holy, every one of them, and the Lord is with them. Why do you set yourselves above the Lord's assembly?' (Numbers 16:3)

In other words they are saying, 'Who do you think you are? What gives you the right to set yourselves up as leaders, and to tell us what to do and how to behave. These people are holy enough. Get off their backs and leave them alone. On what grounds do you assume the right to lead us?' This of course is a perfectly reasonable question to ask. On what grounds does anyone have the right to assume leadership amongst the people of God? How does anyone receive the authority to lead and expect others to cooperate?

The ringleader of this group of men was a man named Korah. He was a Levite. The Levites were already given privileged position in that 'the God of Israel has separated you from the rest of the Israelite community and brought you near himself to do the work at the Lord's tabernacle, and to stand before the community and minister to them.' Now it is true that every priest was to be a Levite, though not every Levite was to be a priest. So far, only Aaron, the brother of Moses, has been given the position as priest. Korah's problem was that in not being content with the role God had already given him as a Levite, he was demanding the particular privilege and responsibility of the priesthood too.

Moses' diagnosis of this is interesting: 'It is against the Lord that you and all your followers have banded together. Who is Aaron that you should grumble against him?' (Numbers 16:11) The rebellion is not against Aaron, or against Moses, but against God.

Attacking God's People To Attack God

If someone wishes to attack God, what do they do? They cannot literally attack God, for he is invisible and there is nothing to hit! I will tell you what they will do. They will attack his people, they will turn their attention to those who are known as his men and his women. If God has given you position and a measure of influence, and you seek to honour the Lord Jesus and to walk humbly with him, then do not be surprised if you come under attack. 'Everyone who wants to live a godly life in Christ Jesus will be persecuted.' (2 Timothy 3:12) This is not because a godly life is despicable, for the reverse is true, but because godliness is the tangible expression of God. If someone wants to hurt God, they must attack that which expresses him.

That is why we must not take persecution too personally, unless of course we are foolishly provoking antagonism on our own account. The persecution of the church through its history has been the persecution of Christ. To one of the earliest opponents of the Christian church, Saul of Tarsus, Jesus asked: 'Saul, Saul, why do you persecute me?' (Acts 9:4) Saul, who was spending his time 'breathing out murderous threats against the Lord's disciples' (Acts 9:1) was flabbergasted! 'Who are you Lord?' Saul asked. How could he attack Christ and not even know who he is? Very simply, by attacking his church, which is his body. The Lord Jesus Christ is incarnate in the world in the body his Father gave him on the Day of Pentecost. That body consists of all those who have entered into relationship with him. He is the head, his Spirit is the life, and we are the individual members that comprise the body. (*See* 1 Corinthians 12) Therefore an attack on the body is an attack on Christ, and the reason why there might be an attack on the body is not because there is a conflict with the church but a conflict with Christ himself. This is in effect what Moses diagnosed.

God had to reassure Samuel of this when the people rebelled and demanded a king so as to be like the nations around about them. Samuel, as their leader, was depressed and hurt and God said to him, 'It is not you they have rejected, but they have rejected me as their king.' (1 Samuel 8:7) In other words, 'Samuel, please do not take this personally. You inevitably take the brunt of their rebellion for you are the physical target. But the people do not have a controversy with you they have a controversy with me.'

I do not want to negate legitimate criticism. We must always take our critics seriously in the sense that we must consider that they may be right. If they are, then we should listen to them and be thankful for them, then in humility we may do what is appropriate to make correction. However, there will be that opposition that is directed against God. It is fundamentally an expression of rebellion against him and we must treat it as such.

We do not need to vindicate ourselves or God. He will do both in his own time.

God's Judgement

Without going in to the details, God subsequently brought a severe judgement on the leaders of this rebellion. The ringleaders all perished in an earthquake that swallowed them up and buried them alive, and their cohorts were destroyed when 'fire came out from the Lord and consumed the two hundred and fifty men.' (Numbers 16:35)

Amazingly, the whole nation then 'grumbled against Moses and Aaron. "You have killed the Lord's people," they said.' (Numbers 16:41) Moses and Aaron could hardly win! The people have first accused them of taking responsibilities that many others could equally have done, and now that God has expressed himself in such a dramatic judgement upon the rebellion, those who remain accuse them of being responsible for their destruction!

God promises to put an end to this continued rebellion and sends another round of judgement against the people. This time it was a plague. Moses sent Aaron to intercede on behalf of the people to prevent it, 'Take your censor and put incense in it, along with fire from the altar, and hurry to the assembly to make atonement for them. Wrath has come out from the Lord, the plague has started . . . Aaron offered the incense and made atonement for them. He stood between the living and the dead, and the plague stopped. But 14,700 people died from the plague, in addition to those who died because of Korah.' (Numbers 16:46–49) This is a horrific story of rebellion and judgement followed by more rebellion and more judgement. It is all about the issue of knowing whom God has called to lead and to perform particular functions in accordance with his will.

How then do we know that God has called someone to a task? Do we simply take people's own word for it? Is there some test we can apply?

Evidence Of God's Calling

This is where Aaron's staff comes into play. God declares he will demonstrate once and for all whom he has called to the priesthood 'and I will rid myself of this constant grumbling against you by the Israelites.' (Numbers 17:5)

Moses is to get twelve staffs, one to represent each of the twelve tribes of Israel. On each staff is to be written the name of the person to whom it belongs. Representing the tribe of Levi was to be Aaron's staff. The staff was not simply a walking stick carried for convenience, but it represented the authority, status and ministry of that tribe. This had always been its meaning. Jacob, in blessing his sons before he died, said to Judah: 'The sceptre will not depart from Judah, nor the ruler's staff from between his feet until it comes to whom it belongs.' (Genesis 49:10) This is clearly a Messianic statement. The staff of Judah, the 'ruler's staff' would come into the hand of the Messiah, the 'lion of the tribe of Judah.' (Revelation 5:5) This of course was the whole issue at stake at this time. The people had been saying 'we can do the job just as well as Aaron and Moses' and the object of the exercise was to show whom God had chosen and the evidence of his choice.

All twelve staffs were taken into the tabernacle and placed in the Most Holy Place before the ark of the covenant. Only the priest was eligible to enter the Most Holy Place, and therefore it was appropriate, in establishing who had been called to the priesthood, to place the staffs in the place only the priest should go. Having done so, the owners were sent home and the staffs were left overnight 'before the Lord.'

The next day 'Moses entered the Tent of the Testimony and saw that Aaron's staff, which represented the house of Levi, had not only sprouted but had budded, blossomed and produced almonds.' (Numbers 17:8)

What was the evidence that Aaron was the man God had chosen? It was very simple. *There was life in his staff.* The staff had sprouted, budded, blossomed and produced almonds. This was something supernatural. The life in the staff had a divine origin. You could not explain Aaron's staff by Aaron, you could only explain Aaron's staff by God. All other eleven staffs could be explained by their owner. In fact there was nothing to explain because nothing happened to any of them. Only with Aaron's staff did something happen, and that was supernatural. God did it.

When God Calls God Does It

To accomplish his work in the world, God is not looking for volunteers! He is looking for those who are willing to make themselves totally available, with no strings attached, for his instructions and the implementation of his plans.

God is committed only to his own programme. He is not committed to yours or to mine, however great, noble and impressive they may appear to be. Korah and his friends may well have volunteered to fulfil the priesthood and humanly speaking may have been as capable and qualified as anyone else. God was totally unimpressed by that. God is not committed to our enthusiasm, he is committed only to our obedience.

Occasionally I have been in situations when people have been challenged to 'volunteer for the mission field' or 'volunteer to teach a Sunday School class' or 'volunteer to do the youth work' or some other similar idea. God doesn't want volunteers. It is not the criteria. He wants us to be available, and it is right to challenge people regarding their willingness to do anything, to go anywhere, to pay any price so that God's will may be done and his interests furthered, and to call people to 'present their bodies as a living sacrifice.' (Romans 12:1) But to engage in any work for God on my own initiative, or simply to 'do my bit', without any concern for his will and his purposes, is not only foolish but sinful!

The prophet Azariah once made an interesting statement to Asa, King of Judah. He said: 'The Lord is with you when you are with him.' (2 Chronicles 15:2) How then am I to know God is with me? Very simply, by making sure I am with him. To ask God to 'be with me' is a totally redundant prayer. How often we pray and ask God to 'be with us' in this or that situation. We do not need to ask him to be with us, we need to make sure we are with him. Our prayer needs to be: 'Help me to be with you today,' and if I make it my business to be with him, he will make it his business to be with me. Jesus said something very similar: 'Where I am, my servant also will be.' (John 12:26) Do not reverse this and say 'Where his servant is, there Jesus will be.' The pace is not set by the servant but by the Lord. His promise 'surely I am with you always, to the very end of the age' (Matthew 28:20) is in the context of his final and great commission to the disciples immediately prior to his ascension. If they act under his authority and implement his programme of making disciples of all nations, then 'I am with you always.' Of course he is always with us in the sense of his being omnipresent. In that sense we ask with David 'where can I go from your Spirit? Where can I flee from your presence?' (Psalm 139:7) He is always with us. This promise of presence with his obedient disciples speaks of presence in power and in his mighty working.

However, there is more at stake than simply his presence. It is the fact that 'The one who calls you is faithful and he will do it.' (1 Thessalonians 5:19) This is to do with ability. God does not call us to go out and do a job for him, but that he may have a channel through which he may do his work through us. The reason Aaron's staff budded and blossomed is because having been called by God it was God who would take responsibility for the work. God was committed to no other staff in the tabernacle, for no other staff was there by his appointing. If any other man took the role of priest, no matter how sincerely motivated, enthusiastic or well qualified, God had no commitment to work. Aaron was his choice, and through Aaron he would work.

This does not mean that God is committed to a select few people. If you happen to be one of them, that is fine. If you do not, tough! He is committed to everyone of us, for he has plans for everyone of us. God's strategy involves every one of his children, and without exception, it is through every one of us that he will work.

The apostle Paul describes the church as being the body of Christ. Christ is the Head, and every true Christian is a member of that body, with no exceptions. He makes two basic statements about the body that every Christian needs to appreciate. *We are different*, for all have separate functions and differing abilities, but *we are dependent* for none should operate in isolation or independence.

67

'There are different kinds of gifts, but the same Spirit. There are different kinds of service, but the same Lord. There are different kinds of working, but the same God works all of them in all men.' (1 Corinthians 12:4–6) For that reason I must never try to be like someone else, or worse, insist that others must be like me. God has made us different and he has called us to different functions.

He illustrates this by saying how that the 'foot should not say "Because I am not a hand I do not belong to the body" and the ear should not say "because I am not an eye I do not belong to the body".' The fact is, states Paul, 'God has arranged the parts of the body, every one of them, just as he wanted them to be.' (1 Corinthians 12:18)

Now I can imagine the foot feeling that the hand is superior to itself, and is treated with much greater dignity than the foot ever is. The foot is stuffed into a sock first thing in the morning and stays there most of the day, whereas the hand is out in the fresh air all the time! People shake the hand, they never shake the foot! We put rings on fingers but never on toes! The foot could quite easily conclude that its differences from the hand make it inferior!

The ear could also feel the same about the eye. People look you in the eye, they never look you in the ear! They may comment on the colour of your eyes, but they never talk about the colour of your ears – and if they do, they are normally being rude! The ear could very easily think itself inferior.

Yes, the body is made up of lots of different parts, and God engineered it that way and made every part important for its own function. Similarly, Paul is stating that there are many different roles and gifts that God has ordained within his body the church. It is true that some roles may have a higher profile than others, but it is not true to conclude them to therefore be more important or more significant.

We Are All Dependent

It is equally true that although we are different we are dependent. 'The eye cannot say to the hand, "I don't need you!" And the head cannot say to the feet "I don't need you!" ' Every part of the body needs every other part. Jesus Christ is not working only through individuals, he is working through his church as a corporate body. Individuals make up the church, but it is the body we have been baptised into by the Holy Spirit, and it is as a body that he works, each in mutual dependence upon the other. There can be no such thing as 'lone rangers' in the work of God. Aaron was not a lone ranger, though he had a lone function. The issue at stake with his staff was not whether God had work for the other tribes to do, or the other members of the tribe of Levi who had not been given the priesthood, but whether they were all equally qualified to do the work God had given Aaron to do. Of course they were not, but God did have other work for them to do.

It is true that some aspects of the work of God have a higher profile than other aspects. Aaron's priesthood would be a case in point. We might then mistakingly conclude that the work was therefore more important and paid bigger rewards on the day of judgement! I am concerned as I travel around to sometimes get the feeling that some Christians think themselves inferior to others, and more sadly, that some may be tempted to think themselves superior. Neither is true.

I once received a letter from a man in the East of England saying they had recently baptized four teenage boys in their church. In the course of the service all four had given testimony as to how they became Christians, and in each case I had apparently led them to Christ. He was writing this because he thought I would be encouraged to know it, and I was. It was wonderful to read. Then he listed the names of each of the four, but the names meant nothing to me. I did not know one of them. I realized there was something imbalanced about this, which highlighted a problem that often exists. Although I am delighted to have had some role in these people coming to Christ, the way they recorded their testimonies that night is not the way God sees it. I am not sure when it was they had come to Christ, but presumably at some meeting at which I had been speaking. But that was the extent of my role. Long before that, however, almost certainly someone had been praying for them, probably witnessing to them, maybe opening their homes to them. Perhaps they were part of a youth group, and before that, part of a Sunday School programme. Someone had brought them to that meeting, and someone had followed them up afterwards. I really don't know the details. But, when they stood to give testimony and said 'Charles Price led me to Christ', God saw it very differently. My part was one small link in a long chain, and in many senses it was the easiest link.

Paul combatted this same mistaken estimate of things when writing to the Corinthian church. 'What is Apollos and what is Paul? Only servants through whom you came to believe—as the Lord has assigned to each his task. I planted the seed, Apollos watered it, but God made it grow. So neither he who plants nor he who waters is anything, but only God who makes things grow. The man who plants and the man who waters have one purpose, and each will be rewarded according to his own labour.' (1 Corinthians 3:5–8)

Do not be unduly elated by visible evidence of God's fruit, and do not be unduly discouraged if you cannot see much evidence of fruit that relates directly to your own obedience to God. It is not the apparent fruit that is of prime concern, it is the root from which the fruit derives that must be your concern. If the root is right and you are living in dependency upon Christ, then the fruit will look after itself, whether it seems visible to you or not.

The Root Is More Important Than The Fruit

The fact that God has called you, and is therefore using you will be expressed ultimately in fruit, 'the sprouting, the budding, the blossom and the almonds'. Of this we can be confident, even when the fruit is not as fully evident as we may like to see. Notice that on Aaron's staff was each stage of the process that leads to mature fruit. Some parts just beginning to *sprout*, some formed into *buds*, others in full *blossom* and yet others ripened into *almonds*. From some people's lives will come the sprouting, the initial evidence of life, so that from others may come the budding and yet others the blossom until finally the full effect comes into being, the almonds. Paul wrote: 'I planted the seed, Apollos watered it...The man who plants and the man who waters have one purpose and each will be rewarded according to his labour.' (1 Corinthians 3:6–8) Each is different, but each is dependent.

Whatever God has called you to do, rest assured, there will be fruit that will please God. You may not be able to measure or tabulate it, but you can rest your head on the pillow each night and know that he has been at work. Do not try to measure the value or significance of your work by its apparent *results*, but by its *cause*. If you do what you do because God put you there, then you can afford to go for forty years like Jeremiah and not see any tangible evidence of success. But like Jeremiah, it is not how people respond to what you say, but the origin of what you say that is important. When Jeremiah complained to God that he did not know what to say, 'The Lord reached out his hand and touched my mouth and said to me, "Now I have put my words in your mouth." ' (Jeremiah 1:9)

Then Jeremiah knew that people didn't have to respond in order for him to know he had done what is right. The people didn't respond and Jeremiah, human as he was, became a discouraged man. He even died discouraged, but more than two and a half thousand years later we are benefiting today from the words of Jeremiah, and through his obedience we still hear God speak to us. This is the fruit, and he could be sure of it, not in measuring the immediate results of his ministry but in the cause from which his ministry sprang.

Other men wanted Aaron's ministry. Place a staff in their hands, they might be able to use it impressively. But take the man away from the staff and the staff is lifeless and fruitless. Take Aaron away from his staff, put him to bed for a good night's sleep, and in the morning it has sprouted, budded, blossomed and produced fruit. It is alive with supernatural life. Take a man God has called and remove him from his ministry and it will continue to bear fruit. Take a man God has not called, and put him in the ministry, and everything that happens will be related only to his own ability. Take him away and the work will die with him. Take him away and the work collapses in a dead heap. Only the life of God perpetuates the work of God.

After a visit I once made to a school in the West of England, a sixteen-year-old-girl who had been in one of the classes I have visited, stopped me in the break time and asked me how she could become a Christian. She attended the evening meetings I was conducting in a local church, and was unmistakably born again. Since then she has grown from strength to strength in her Christian life. She had no church connections, and I asked her one day if anything had taken place in her past to prepare her for what I had said to her class that particular morning. It seems unusual for someone to come from nowhere to Christ just like that.

She told me that as a child she had been sent to a Sunday School led by one elderly man in a little green hut near her home. He had died when she was only seven or eight, and no one had taken on the responsibility of the Sunday School so it had been closed. She had no real involvement with Christians since.

I later discovered that the elderly man had stubbornly insisted on running his very small Sunday School, despite having no help from any others, because he was convinced it was the will of God for him to do so. In the years he did it, he never saw any real results, which was partly why it was not continued by others after he died. But God had called him, and consequently, there was life in his work. Long after he died I am convinced that the good seed he had sown in that girl's heart had germinated and sprung to life. Take away the man and finish the work, but the 'staff' was alive and years later it bore fruit.

Where then did Aaron get his staff from? How do you get a life and ministry that lives and bears fruit? The answer to that is vital to our spiritual health and well-being. It also happens to be very interesting and we will explore it in the next chapter.

6: What Is That In Your Hand?

We have looked at Aaron's staff and discovered that when it was taken from him and placed in the tabernacle overnight it sprouted, budded, blossomed and produced almonds. The next morning the eleven staffs placed with it, representing the other eleven tribes of Israel, remained exactly as they had been the night before. They were lifeless and barren. Others had wanted the ministry God had given to Aaron, and God was demonstrating that he is not committed to anyone else's ideas, dedication or enthusiasm, he is committed only to his own programme. It was God who had called Aaron and it was God who infused his ministry with supernatural life. Take Aaron away from his staff and his staff still bears fruit. The life did not come from Aaron, it came from God.

Where then did Aaron get his staff from? Why is he assured of this kind of fruitfulness? How can we enjoy a life that is certain of being productive and so give a channel for the activity of God?

I find the answer to this question to be fascinating. Aaron got his staff from Moses! Moses gave it to him before they left Egypt. Before we look at the circumstances in which that took place, we need to discover where Moses got his staff from in the first place. To discover that we go back to his encounter with God at the burning bush.

When God called Moses at the burning bush and told him to go and bring the Israelites out of Egypt, there came a point in the conversation when God said to him: ' "What is that in your hand?" "A staff" he replied. The Lord said, "Throw it on the ground." ' (Exodus 4:2) This staff was the tool of Moses' trade. For the past forty years he has been a shepherd in the Midian desert, and the staff in his hand represented his whole livelihood. This was his vocation, this brought him his income, from this derived his security and that of his family. Now the Lord is telling him to throw it on the ground, to cast it down before the burning bush where God is present.

'Moses threw it on the ground and it became a snake, and he ran from it.' This is a very dramatic picture. The staff Moses had carried in his hand, the symbol of his work, of his security, of his income, of his livelihood, now thrown down before God has become a snake, 'and he ran from it'. This harmless staff that he has carried in his hand all these years, that he has shepherded his flocks with, that his children have played games with, that he has placed by his bed when he went to sleep at night, is now something from which he runs. It has become a snake and it will do him harm!

When God does something there is always a message and purpose in it. This was not just a magical trick to impress Moses, and later with which Moses would impress the Egyptian leaders. It is true that this incident was repeated before the leaders of Israel and then before Pharaoh, but it did not impress Pharaoh, for 'the Egyptian magicians also did the same things by their secret arts. Each one threw down his staff and it became a snake.' (Exodus 7:11) True as it is that this was an immediate demonstration of God's power to Moses, at the same time there was more significant meaning to this event.

In Egyptian worship, the serpent played a prominent role. I have been to the Egyptian Museum in Cairo and viewed the relics from ancient times, as far back and further than the time of Moses. In the long history of

75

Egyptian civilization, snakes are conspicuous by their presence, particularly the cobra. It appears repeatedly in its most dangerous stance, its head raised vertically above the ground, its neck flattened, ready to strike. This was the object of Egyptian idolatory, superstition and fear. Moses is about to take on the might of the Egyptian empire, the most progressive, civilized and dominant power of the day, and it will be braced for attack.

But the snake has a history that predates and postdates the mighty Egyptian empire. The serpent made its first appearance in the Garden of Eden as Satan incarnate. He makes his last appearance at the end of Revelation when an angel, 'seized the dragon, the ancient serpent, who is the devil, or Satan, and bound him for a thousand years. He threw him into the Abyss, and locked and sealed it over him.' (Revelation 20:2) Satan's first and his last guise is as the serpent. Snakes today figure in occultic and demonic activities. They represent something evil, sinister and Satanic.

To his horror, as Moses threw his staff to the ground, he discovered it could turn so quickly into a snake.

Take It By The Tail

With the snake writhing on the ground and Moses making certain to keeps his distance, God gave him a very surprising instruction. 'Then the Lord said to him, "Reach out your hand and take it by the tail." ' (Exodus 4:4) I don't know how much you know about snakes, but one thing you never do with a snake is take it by the tail! If you take a snake by the tail it's head will slide up its body, it will strike you and bite you, you may begin to feel a little dizzy, you may fall over, you may start to go blue and you may die! If you take a snake at all, you take it by the head. That, you see, is the dangerous part, and you always need to be in control of the dangerous part.

Unless it is a constrictor and likely to wrap itself around you and squeeze you to death, its tail is perfectly harmless. It is the mouth that is the source of the venom and it is therefore the head you need to have under control!

Moses knew that. Living as he did in the Midian desert he would encounter snakes as a regular if not daily event. He would almost certainly have killed many during his years as a shepherd. Now God gives him this strange instruction to take the snake by its tail.

What is God saying to him? What is the meaning behind this enacted parable? I suggest he is saying this: 'Moses, I want you to know the potential of the staff you carry in your hand. You may think it is useful and perfectly harmless, but I want you to know it can suddenly be a snake. That good and useful staff can potentially harbour danger, a danger that could destroy you. Thrown on the ground before me, it has been exposed for what it potentially is. Your seemingly harmless staff may become a harbour for the devil himself.

'But now take it by the tail. I am putting the staff back in your hand. You take the tail, which is the harmless part, and I will look after the head, which is the dangerous part.'

The first time God addresses Satan in the Bible is in the Garden of Eden. Addressing him as the serpent he affirms enmity between him and the seed of the woman, the Lord Jesus, and states of him: 'He will crush your head.' (Genesis 3:17) That will be a fatal blow, and Christ will administer it. Dealing with the serpent's head is God's responsibility not ours.

The Staff Of God

As Moses takes the snake by the tail 'it turned back into a staff in his hand.' (Exodus 4:4) Now he had the staff back in his hand again, but was it the same staff? No, there was a fundamental difference. 'Moses took his wife and

sons, put them on a donkey and started back to Egypt.
And he took the *staff of God* in his hand.' (Exodus) This
is now the '*staff of God*'. It was of course the same piece
of wood that Moses had carried before his encounter at
the burning bush. When he brought it home that night
his family would recognize the familiar notches and
carvings and the shape of its handle. But it was a different
staff. Previously it had been the staff of Moses. Now it
was the staff of God, and what a difference that made!

Later God would tell Moses to stretch his staff over the
Red Sea, and when he did so, the waters opened. When
they went into the desert and ran out of water, God told
Moses to strike the rock with his staff, and water gushed
out. In battle with the Amalakites, Joshua led the army
into battle whilst Moses stood 'on the top of the hill with
the staff of God in his hand.' (Exodus 17:9) As long as
Moses kept up his hands the Israelites were winning, but
whenever he lowered them the Amalakites were winning.
Eventually Aaron and his son Hur came to his aid, one
holding up each hand that the staff might remain lifted
and Israel prevail in the battle. This is some staff! It used
to be the staff of Moses, good for rounding up sheep. Now
it is the staff of God and miracles abound. God specifically
instructed Moses: 'Take this staff in your hand so you can
perform miraculous signs with it.' (Exodus 4:17) This was
to be the tool of his new trade, the means whereby God
would perform mighty acts.

Moses' Staff Becomes Aaron's Staff

The reason this is of interest in our present study is that
it seems it was Moses' staff that became Aaron's staff. Prof.
F.F. Bruce points this out in his article on 'Aaron's Staff'
in the *New Bible Dictionary**. After the incident of the staff
budding, Moses was told to 'Put back Aaron's staff in front

**New Bible Dictionary*, Second Edition. Published by IVP.

of the Testimony, to be kept as a sign to the rebellious.' (Numbers 17:18) A little while later, Moses is told to take the staff and speak to the rock at Kadesh and 'it will pour out its water'. (Numbers 20:7) He then 'took the staff from the Lord's presence', meaning the Most Holy Place where Aaron's staff had been placed. He then struck the rock twice with it in disobedience, having been commanded to simply speak to the rock. The point I am making is that the staff of Moses, used to strike the rock in Numbers 20 was the staff of Aaron, which had budded in Numbers 17, and then been placed in the tabernacle.

It also seems that right after the encounter at the burning bush, Moses and Aaron shared the same staff when performing miracles in Egypt. You will remember that because of Moses' reluctance to go back to Egypt and be able to speak to Pharaoh, Aaron was sent as his 'prophet'. It was not Moses who performed the first miracle before Pharaoh, but his brother. 'Aaron threw his staff down in front of Pharaoh and his officials, and it became a snake.' (Exodus 7:10) For the first of the ten plagues against Egypt, God told Moses: ' ''Go to Pharaoh in the morning as he goes out to the water. Wait on the bank of the Nile to meet him, and take in your hand the staff that was changed into a snake . . .'' The Lord said to Moses, ''Tell Aaron, 'Take *your* staff and stretch out your hand over the waters of Egypt' . . . and all the water was changed into blood.'' ' (Exodus 7:14–21) It is apparently Moses' staff that is used by Aaron and becomes identified as Aaron's staff.

What Is In Your Hand?

This all becomes pointedly relevant. If we want to know where Aaron got is staff from, if we are going to discover how to live a life that is fruitful, then it must begin with God asking: 'What is that in your hand?', and with our willingness to 'throw it down' before him in complete surrender. It may be that in your hand is something as useful and as harmless as Moses' staff was to him, but in *your* hand, under *your* control, it may become a harbour for the snake.

May I ask you, '*What is that in your hand?*' You may say 'It is my job.' You may have worked hard to get where you are. It may have occupied a lot of time, sweat and trouble, but you are finally making it. It means a lot to you. But will you drop it before God? In your hand it could be dangerous. In your hand the snake might make his inroads. But you drop it at the feet of God, he may give it you back as he gave Moses his staff back, but you will take it by the tail and God will crush its head. He will take care of the snake, and your job will become *the job of God*, as Moses' staff became *the staff of God*. It will be the same job, but under different management. He will do things in your place of work that will defy any other adequate explanation other than that God is doing it.

'*What is that in your hand?*' You may say, 'My studies. I have ambitions and I am working towards fulfilling them. I will soon be qualified.' This may be true and good. But will you drop it before God? Will you lay it at his feet and give him the right to take it away if that is his will, or to give it back to you if that fulfils his plan? Legitimate and good as your studies and ambitions may be, in *your* hand they will be only *your* studies and ambitions, and they may contain the snake. Give them to God and you have nothing to fear. If they are right and he gives them back to you, you will hold them by the tail and he will be taking care of the potentially dangerous part. They will become '*God's studies*' equipping you for a life that will be effective and fruitful.

'*What is that in your hand?*' You say 'My money. I have earned every penny and I use it wisely.' Will you 'drop it' before God? There are perhaps few places where Satan so easily finds a lodging-place than in our money and in our attitude to it. Dropped before God he may give it you back, but you take it only by the tail. It will become 'God's money'. You do not know what he will do with it that will release his life and produce his fruit. As 'your money' it might be dangerous. As 'God's money' it will be effective.

'What is that in your hand?' You may say 'My family'. This is legitimate, right and a gift of God. But if you are a father or a mother, will you drop your children at the feet of God and give them back to him. You can be sure he will give them back to you, but you will hold them only by 'the tail'. God may do what he will with your family, and there may be rough times or tough times, there may be sadness or bereavement but this is 'God's family', and he has a purpose in all that he permits. The inroads Satan would make into your home will require that he battles with God.

'What is that in your hand?' You may say 'My church responsibilities. I am an elder, a deacon, part of the leadership. I teach a Sunday School class. I lead the youth work. I preach the Gospel.' Will you drop it at the feet of God? Will you surrender to him every role you occupy? Will you throw down every hidden agenda you may hold for your church and seek only to know and do the will of God? Fail to do that and you may lead the church, teach a Bible class or occupy the pulpit every Sunday, but it will be 'your church' and you will preach 'your sermons' giving 'your ideas' to 'your Sunday School class' and they will become open territory to the snake. Lay them at his feet, and as God instructs you, take them again but only by the tail. This will become God's church, God's Sunday School class, and you will be God's elder, God's preacher and there will be life and power and fruit in your work.

Like Moses and Aaron this does not mean life will be easy, for you will be taken to the front line of spiritual warfare, needing every drop of wisdom and

81

resourcefulness, but the Pharaohs won't frighten you, the Red Sea won't hold you back, the drought won't deter you, the Amalakites will not beat you, for you have in your hand what Moses had in his hand, the *'staff of God'*. It is God's business, perpetrating only his interests. As you hold it only by the tail, it is God who will deal with the head of the serpent. Then, if for some reason you are taken away from your work, you no longer preach in the church, you do not teach the Sunday School class and you cease to be a leader among the people, the staff will 'sprout, bud, blossom and produce almonds' long after you are gone.

But if you want to keep it in your own hand, then you may keep it! God will not force the issue, he will not twist your arm or put a bomb under you. You are as Godly as you really want to be. But I must warn you, if you keep the staff in your own hand, you will keep the snake as well! And you do not know when he will choose to uncoil and strike. You do not know when it will be, whether in your job, in your studies, in your use of money, in your family or in your church that the 'ancient serpent called the devil' (Revelation 12:9) will strike and wound. The sad thing will be, that you have given him access.

This is the staff of Aaron. He got it from Moses. Moses got it from God. It is really the staff of God. Whose staff is in your hand?

7: Why God Gave The Law

The original contents of the ark were the stone tablets of the covenant, given by God to Moses on Mount Sinai, and on which were written the ten commandments. Good as we would agree these ten commandments to be, they are of course, totally unrealistic! Nobody has, nobody can and nobody will ever keep them. Without knowing anything else about you personally, were I to meet you, I would be quite prepared to look you straight in the eye and say to you: 'You have broken the law of God.' You would not consider me to be impertinent, because you know it is true, and you know I would know it is true. In fact you would probably look me back in the eye and say, 'And so have you,' and you would be right!

Why then has God given to us a set of rules that we are unable to keep? That would seem rather unreasonable, don't you think? If you have ever been involved in making rules, you will know that a basic principle in making rules is that any rule people can't keep is a bad rule! If you make rules people can't keep, you are asking for trouble, and it would be your fault! Why then has God given to us a set of rules that no one is able to keep?

I believe it will be of great value to us to try to understand this, for in doing so we will unlock some fundamental issues in God's purpose for man, with important repercussions that we need to know.

The law is not just an arbitrary set of rules, motivated

primarily by man's need of some clear instruction on how to behave. It is true that laws serve this purpose, but were that to be their primary function, they would be unrealistic, unworkable and inadequate. When the Pharisees reduced the law to that level they had a problem, and had to introduce so many additions to bring it to what they considered a reasonable and workable level. The law has far deeper significance than to be simply a set of rules.

There are three aspects of the law at which we will look. Firstly we will look at the *Purpose Of The Law*, and ask the question: Why did God give a law that is so high in its demands, no one can keep it?

Secondly we will look at the *Effect Of The Law*, and ask the question: What does the law actually do for us?

Thirdly we will look at a statement of Jesus in which he said 'I have not come to abolish the law, but to fulfil it.' (Matthew 5:17) We will think about the *Fulfilment Of The Law*, and ask the question: How does Jesus make it work?

The Purpose Of The Law

Firstly, then, we will ask the question, Why did God give a law that no one could keep? Perhaps you have never thought about this before, but how did God decide what the law should be? Why did God give ten commandments? Why did he not give six or twenty? What determined what those commandments should be? Were they arbitrarily chosen, or is there some criteria that made it necessary for each to be included?

To answer that question we must look at two verses in the New Testament that describe what sin is. Before we look at them, I will remind you that the word 'sin' literally means 'to miss the mark'. I understand the word was originally used in archery. If someone took an arrow and aimed it at a target but missed, it was described as 'sin'.

If the target was missed by an inch, it was called sin. If missed my a yard, it was called sin. If missed by a mile, it was called sin. By how far the target had been missed was irrelevant to whether it was sin, for to sin was to miss the mark. That is why 'sin' in the Bible is not so much a measurement of how bad we are, but of how good we are not! To sin is to miss the mark, whether by an inch, a foot, a yard or a mile. There is a sense in which God is not particularly concerned with how bad we are. Of course there are different kinds of sins with different repercussions in our lives, and worse, in the lives of others, but the substance of sin is to have missed the mark. By how far we have missed may have importance but it is secondary. If you miss a bus by one minute, five minutes or one hour, the timing is really irrelevant. The issue is that you have missed the bus.

If sin is to 'miss the mark', then sin in itself is not an absolute! Sin is relative. It is the mark which has been missed that is absolute, and we can only measure and recognize sin in the light of the target that has been missed. If you call someone a 'sinner' they may be outraged at your impertinence, and for good reason, for they will never understand sin unless they understand the target that their sin has missed. It is the target which is absolute, and the target that we must understand. Fail to understand the target, and all classification of sin will at some time appear unreasonable.

Although there are many, many things that may be described in the Bible as sins, there are only two definitions that apply to all sin, and which mark the target against which all sin must be defined. The first is a statement by John in his first epistle, and the second by Paul in the book of Romans.

John writes: 'Everyone who sins breaks the law; in fact, sin is lawlessness.' (1John 3:4) If to sin is to 'miss the target', John declares the target to be the law of God. Every sin that a person may commit, irrespective of what they have actually done, will involve a breaking of the law, for the law represents the mark that has been missed.

This does not in itself answer our question as to why the law is what it is. If the law alone by its very standard has decreed what constitutes sin, then why did God not lower the standard a little and make it easier? We are still left with the same basic question as to why its standard is so high.

However, keep John's verse in mind and compare it with a statement of Paul in the book of Romans where he also defines what sin involves: 'For all have sinned and fall short of the glory of God.' (Romans 3:23)

Here is a second definition of sin. Paul is saying that every time a person sins, no matter what the nature of their sin may be, the mark they have missed is the 'glory of God'. Before we define what that is, let us put those two verses together. If John writes that the mark we miss each time we sin is the '*law*' and Paul declares that the mark we miss each time we sin is the '*glory of God*', then the '*law of God*' and the '*glory of God*' must equal each other and represent the same thing. Therefore, if we are going to understand why the law of God is what it is, we must ask another question: *What is the glory of God?*

The word 'glory' occurs in Scripture with slight variation of meaning, depending on its context. However, essentially the *glory of God* is the *character of God*. The *New Bible Dictionary* states that the glory of God 'denotes the revelation of God's being, nature and presence . . . In the New Testament . . . its chief use is to describe the revelation of the character and the presence of God.'* It is essentially a revelation of the character of God.

It is the kind of thing John had in mind when writing in his gospel of Jesus he declared: 'The Word became flesh and made his dwelling among us. We have seen his glory, *New Bible Dictionary*, published by IVP.

the glory of the One and Only, who came from the Father, full of grace and truth.' (John 1:16) When John states that 'we have seen his glory' he is not meaning that there was a visible light about six inches above Jesus' head, as artists have sometimes portrayed! He is saying that in the character of Jesus we saw the character of God. In practical terms he is stating that those who were contemporaries of Jesus as a boy in Nazareth saw in his behaviour the moral character of God. As he played with his friends, kicked a ball up the street, went hiding in the woods or hunting in the hills, as he responded to his parents and respected his brothers and sisters at home, they saw in him what God was like. When he began to work in his father's carpenter's shop, the way he did his work, the way he payed his bills on time, the way he invoiced accurately for the work that he had done, the way he treated his colleagues, all demonstrated for anyone to see what God is like. When he began his public ministry, and began to preach to the crowds, the way he treated a woman everyone else would be embarrassed to be seen with, the way he crossed the road to touch the leper no one had touched for years, the way he made himself the friend of outcasts and sinners, the way he let the children climb all over him when his disciples would prefer to get them off their hands, John is declaring 'We saw what God is like!' This is the glory of God, it is the moral character of God. 'The Son is the radiance of God's glory and the exact representation of his being.' (Hebrews 1:3) If we want to know what God is like, we look no further than to His Son, 'the exact representation of his being'.

If this was true of Jesus, it was not intended only to be true of Jesus. It was intended in creation to be true of all people. When God first declared his purpose for man he said: 'Let us make man in our image, in our likeness.' (Genesis 1:26) That is not a physical image for God is not a physical being. There can be no such thing as a physical likeness to God, for he has no body. When the Bible says that 'no one has ever seen God' (John 1:18) it is not because he is hiding! It is because there is nothing to see! 'God is spirit.' (John 4:24) Therefore when the Bible declares man to have been made in his 'image' and 'likeness' it is speaking of *his moral likeness*. In the character and behaviour of man was to be seen a perfect portrayal of the character and behaviour of God.

If you or I could have been a fly on the wall in the garden of Eden and had watched the way Adam treated Eve, we would have seen what God is like. If we had observed how Eve treated Adam, we would have seen what God is like. If we watched the way they handled and responded to the animals and birds in the garden, we would have seen what God is like. Being made in his image, if you looked at them, you would have seen the object of which they were the image. You would have seen the character of God!

Then tragedy struck. In his foolishness man sinned and 'fell short of the glory of God'. Now, when you looked at man you did not see what God was like, you saw only a fallen distortion. Adam's fallen condition was reproduced in his children: 'Adam . . . had a son in his own likeness, in his own image; and he named him Seth.' (Genesis 5:3) Adam's likeness had now fallen short of God's likeness, so although Seth showed what Adam was like, he did not now show what God is like. He was fallen. But not only was man fallen, he was lost and confused. He did not know what he should be like anymore because he did not know what God was like anymore!

The Law Of God Represents The Character Of God

If the 'glory of God' is the character of God, and the 'glory of God' is equal to the law of God, then *the law of God was given to reveal the character of God*. That is, if *glory* is equal to *character*, and *glory* is equal to *law*, then *law*

88

is equal to *character*. This is an inescapably logical deduction!

As the eternal purpose of God for man is that he might portray God's image and thus reveal his character, the law was given on Mount Sinai as a revelation of God's character. These were in practical terms designed to be reproduced in man's behaviour.

The law reveals God's character, for it is only in discovering what God is like that man may discover what he is supposed to be like! Hence the law is not an arbitrary set of rules, but a portrayal of the image in which man was first made.

When God said in the law: 'You shall not steal', it was for one primary reason. It was not because stealing is not nice (though it isn't), but because God is not a thief and man was made to be in his image.

When God said in the law: 'You shall not murder,' it was for a far more fundamental reason than simply because it is not good to take another life! It was because God does not murder, and man was made to be in his image.

When God said in the law: 'You shall not commit adultery,' it was because God is totally faithful, and man was made to be in his image. Therefore adultery and true humanity are totally incompatible.

When God said in the law: 'You shall not give false testimony,' it was because God never, ever, tells lies, and therefore, to be in his image, man will never give false witness.

When God said, 'You shall not covet,' it is because God himself is never greedy, and man was made to be in his image.

When God said: 'Six days you shall labour and do all your work, but the seventh day is a Sabbath to the Lord your God,' he explained why. It was because God 'rested on the seventh day'. The reason he did so was not because he was tired, but because his work was finished! The

Sabbath was not instituted to prevent people from burning out through over work, for that was not God's reason for rest. It was to demonstrate that no one is indispensable, and we rest in the total sufficiency and adequacy of God. 'There remains then a Sabbath-rest for the people of God, for anyone who enters God's rest also rests from his own work, just as God did from his.' (Hebrews 4:9–10)

When God said: 'Honour your father and mother, so that you may live long in the land the Lord your God is giving you,' I suggest it was because within the Trinity the Son says of the Father, 'I always do what pleases him,' (John 8:29) and as we were made to be in the image of God, we must honour our father and mother.

The law is not an arbitrary set of rules, designed primarily to create the environment where man could best function in harmony together. That of course will be its consequences, but it is primarily the revelation of the character of God in whose image man was created, and in whose moral likeness he will find his true self.

When Jesus spoke about the law to his disciples in the Sermon On The Mount, he concluded by stating what could only have been a startling command: 'Be perfect therefore as your heavenly Father is perfect.' (Matthew 5:48) Impossible as that would have sounded to his listeners, Jesus in actual fact was saying nothing new! He was reiterating God's statement in the Garden Of Eden: 'Let us make man in our image, in our likeness,' (Genesis 1:26) and endorsed when God gave the law to Moses on Mount Sinai and thus revealed his own character.

This is our first point, and it is vital that we comprehend it. The law was not given as an arbitrary set of rules, but as a revelation of the character of God. Fail to understand that, and we may fail to understand the nature of true salvation, and the full significance of the work of Jesus Christ on our behalf.

The Effect Of The Law

We must now ask a further vital question. If the purpose of the law is to reveal the character of God, what is the effect of the law on man? The answer to that is a fairly straightforward one. *It exposes his failure!*

When Moses came down Mount Sinai having received the law from God, the first commandment said: 'You shall have no other gods before me.' The second added: 'You shall not make for yourself an idol in the form of anything in heaven above or on the earth beneath or in the water below. You shall not bow down to them or worship them.' The reason for this prohibition is very simple. They were to worship no other god because there is no other god! God has no neighbour, he has no competitor, and he has no equal.

When Moses reached the bottom of Sinai, having been away in the mountain for forty days, he discovered to his horror that the children of Israel had pooled their gold, melted it down, and built a golden calf. They were dancing around it and presenting offerings to it as 'the gods who brought you up out of Israel.' (Exodus 32:4) As Moses approached the camp with the law in his hands forbidding this very thing, he was shocked and angry! 'When Moses approached the camp and saw the calf and the dancing, his anger burned and he threw the tablets out of his hands, breaking them to pieces at the foot of the mountain.' (Exodus 32:19) Moses was shocked! God wasn't! God did not learn something new about man. Man learned something new about himself. He discovered he could not be the person he was supposed to be. He was a failure.

Paul wrote: 'I would not have known what sin was except through the law.' (Romans 7:7) In other words, I might be up to my neck in sin, and not only have a clear conscience about it, but be thoroughly enjoying it. But the moment I become aware of the law, its effect is to expose my sin and make me aware of my failure.

On one recent occasion I was visiting Australia for a series of speaking engagements. Leaving England in mid winter I had arrived in New South Wales at the peak of hot summer. Having travelled the twenty-four-hour journey from England I arrived tired, went to bed, and after a good sleep awoke the next morning to drive the sixty or so miles to Sydney where I was to preach. It was a beautiful summer day, and after the cold and wet of England I was thoroughly enjoying the contrasting sun and warmth. Soon I passed through an almost deserted little town. It was fairly early, on a Sunday morning, with little signs of life. As I neared the outskirts of this town, a little way ahead of me, I saw a man in uniform step into the road and order me to stop. I pulled up just beyond him. He came to my window, looked in and asked: 'What speed were you travelling at for the last few hundred metres?'

I felt a little embarrassed, 'I am not sure,' I replied, 'I wasn't actually looking at my speedometer.'

'Then take a guess,' he suggested.

Being used to miles rather than kilometers I did a quick conversion in my mind, 'Seventy-five,' I told him.

'No, you are not even warm,' he responded, 'You were doing ninety-three kilometers per hour. What is the speed limit on this road?'

I confessed I didn't know because I lived in England and wasn't sure of the rules on Australian roads.

'We put up signs!' he told me, 'didn't you read them?'

I confessed I hadn't noticed them, on which he asked me for my driving licence.

'I haven't got it with me,' I told him truthfully, for I had left it back at the place where I was staying.

'Do you know that it is against the law not to have your licence when driving?' he asked.

'No, I don't,' I replied.

By this time I was feeling like a common criminal! As he charged me with my various crimes and then issued a fine for eighty dollars, I drove meekly away feeling rather stung! The interesting thing is that a few minutes before I was driving along with a completely clear conscience. I was enjoying the drive, the scenery, the weather, oblivious to the fact that I was up to my neck in crime, violating various Australian laws! Now the policeman had broken my serenity. He did not make me break the law, he had only revealed to me what the law was, and thereby exposed me for the lawbreaker I clearly was! This is the role of the law of God in our lives too. The law in itself is good, but it makes us aware of our failure and our sin.

The Good Bad News

This is a necessary process. God has to make us aware of our sin, not only in the sense of our moral failure but in the deeper sense of our inability to be what we are supposed to be. Not only must we recognize that what we have done is wrong but that we are weak. We cannot detach what we do from what we are, and treat what we *do* as something independent of what we are! What we *do* is only the symptom. What we *are* is the problem.

We must recognize a distinction between 'sins' and 'sin'. 'Sins' are my behaviour; 'sin' is my nature. It is my sins that expose my sin. What I do reveals what I am. To be aware of my sins yet refuse to face my sin is folly. God makes me aware of my sins in order that he might reveal my sin.

It has often been said that a person is not a sinner because they commit sins, but they commit sins because they are a sinner! To illustrate this point, we could say that a plum tree is not a plum tree because plums grow on it. Rather, plums grow on it because it is a plum tree!

You wouldn't go to your tree a month or two before it is due to bear fruit and wonder if you might have bananas on it this year, or tomatoes! You expect plums for one reason. You planted a plum stone. The plum stone will grow into a plum tree, the plum tree will have a plum nature and all it will be capable of is producing plums! In fact, when you have first planted the tree and it stands only three inches tall, long before it bears its first fruit, you may well say to your neighbour: 'Come and see my plum tree.' Is your confidence in it being a plum tree just wild speculation? Or a prophetic utterance? Of course it is neither! The tree has no choice but to be a plum tree. Neither have you any choice but to be a sinner! It is not the plums that make it the plum tree but the plum tree that makes the plums. It is not your sins that make you the sinner, but your sin that produces the sins.

It is in God's interest to make you and me aware of that as emphatically as possible. If we are only aware of the symptoms, *our sins*, and do not face the cause, *our sin*, we shall only look to Christ to deal with the symptoms, the forgiveness of our sins, rather than their cause, our sin.

The law in exposing our sins is actually doing far more than that. This is something Jesus made very clear on the occasion he talked most comprehensively about the law in his Sermon On The Mount. I imagine some of his hearers received quite a shock that day. They had gone to listen to Jesus preach 'good news'. He had begun his ministry by proclaiming: 'The time has come. The kingdom of God is near. Repent and believe the good news.' (Mark 1:15) If anyone needed good news with plenty of encouragement it was the Israelite nation. Long ago in their history God had given to them a moral law they had been completely unable to keep. If there was one word that could be written across their history it would be the word 'failure'. The historical books of the Old

Testament record the details of that failure. The poetic books weep about their failure. The prophetic books preach about their failure.

Now, the Lord Jesus Christ had come on to the scene preaching 'good news', and many of these people had pricked up their ears with great interest, and made their way up the hillside to listen for themselves to the content of this good news. I imagine that as they walked they speculated with each other about what he would declare to them as so good. I imagine one probably suggested that as the ten commandments had not worked, perhaps there would now only be six! Another suggested that as God had been so difficult to get along with until now, the good news probably was that he was going to soften a little, and not be quite so demanding as he had been in the past! Jesus, seeming to be aware of this kind of conversation among them, announced: 'Do not think that I have come to abolish the Law or the Prophets.' (Matthew 5:17) In other words, there is no embarrassment in heaven about a law they had been unable to keep, nor any apology from God for imposing it upon them. If that wasn't enough he proceeded to make things worse!

He said to them: 'You have heard that it was said to the people long ago, "Do not murder . . ." but I tell you that anyone who is angry with his brother will be subject to judgement.' (Matthew 5:21–22) They may well have agreed that the law against murder was good, but now he is telling them that if they are angry with a brother, even though they never dare put a bullet between his eyes or a knife into his back, they are guilty of murder!

He then said, 'You have heard that it was said, "Do not commit adultery". But I tell you that anyone who looks at a woman lustfully has already committed adultery with her in his heart.' (Matthew 5:27–28) To not commit adultery may have been a reasonable enough law, but now he is saying that if they look lustfully at a woman, even though they may not know her name, find out her address and never dare go and knock on her door, they are guilty of adultery!

This wasn't all! 'You have heard that it was said, "Eye for eye and tooth for tooth," ' and that sounded reasonable enough. 'But I tell you . . . if someone strikes you on the right cheek, turn to him the other also. And if someone wants to sue you and take your tunic, let him have your cloak as well.' (Matthew 5:38–39) Then he added: 'You have heard that it was said, "Love your neighbour and hate your enemy". But I tell you: Love your enemies and pray for those who persecute you.' (Matthew 5:43–44)

I imagine some of these people turned to each other and said: 'This is not good news! This is terrible news! It was bad enough before when we couldn't do these things. Now we can't even think about them!'

What was Jesus doing for these people? He was doing for them what he must do for you and me. He was exposing to them the impossibility of ever being what they are supposed to be by their own resources. He concluded this by saying: 'Be perfect, therefore, as your heavenly father is perfect.' (Matthew 5:48) In other words he was saying: 'Ladies and Gentlemen would you please go home and be as perfect as you know God Himself to be!'

There is only one logical conclusion to draw from this, and that is that the message Jesus preached, and the demand that he made, is humanly impossible and totally out of the question!

Have you ever faced that? Until you have honestly faced the sheer impossibility of the demands of Jesus you will never discover what it is that Jesus himself can do for you. As long as we think we have what it takes, we will never graduate out of failure, for we will renew our efforts, our dedication, our discipline and try again. We will hunt around for new techniques, and new formulas for victory, but we shall return again as a disappointed and despairing people. There is only one logical conclusion to the Sermon on the Mount: The Christian life is impossible! This conclusion is the prelude to the most important discovery you can ever make.

Failure: The Door To Victory

Before we discover what all this is leading to, let me explain that the exposure of our failure and defeat is never for the purpose of humiliating us, of embarrassing us, of condemning us, or of rubbing our noses in our own dirt. Having faced the truth about ourselves, God's desire is to clean us up and change us. A prerequisite to discovering the goodness of the good news is to face honestly the badness of the good news! The good news is the answer to bad news, therefore the extent to which I understand the badness will determine the extent to which I can appreciate and experience the goodness!

Have you ever noticed that a medical doctor is always concerned to know what is wrong with you? You might be forgiven for thinking he has an obsession with it. In fact, it is the only thing he seems to talk to you about? He seems so negative, you wonder if he has a permanent chip on his shoulder! Just suppose that one day you knew you needed some medicine but were fed up with his negative diagnosis of your condition so tried to side-step the issue. You went to his surgery and simply asked him to give you a bottle of pink medicine! He would probably tell you he was not at liberty to just give you some pink medicine, and would rather know what it is that is wrong with you. He might then ask you some very direct and possibly embarrassing questions, and if that wasn't enough he might place his hand on a tender part of your body and ask you to let him know when it hurts, and knowing full well it probably will, he presses against the very spot until you squeal in anguish!

97

Now why is he doing this? Is it because he got out of bed on the wrong side that morning, burned his toast, tripped over the cat and missed his bus, and you happen to have come along at the wrong time and are getting the blunt end of his misery? Well of course not! Having asked you all the questions that expose your symptoms, and then put his hand on the sore part and revealed the pain, he tells you: 'I have some bad news and some good news for you! The bad news is that you are ill! But now I know what is wrong with you, I can tell you what is good for you! The good news is that we have a remedy. It is a bottle of orange medicine.'

The law of God which reveals the character of God, at the same time exposes our sin, our failure and our inability to ever be what we are supposed to be. But this is not the end of the story! This is only the necessary prelude to the third and most important thing. If *the purpose of the law is to reveal the character of God*, and *the effect of the law is to reveal the failure of man*, then we need to discover what Jesus meant when he said of the law: 'I have not come to abolish them but to fulfil them.' (Matthew 5:17) He was saying, 'I have not come to abolish the law as an idea that clearly has not worked and has left you only frustrated! There is no embarrassment in heaven over giving a law you have been unable to keep. I bring you no apology from God for imposing demands you could not fulfil. The law is a revelation of the character of God and that has not changed and will not change. As a revelation of the character of God it is also a revelation of his purpose for man – and that has not changed either. What I have come to do is not to abolish the law but to fulfil the law. I have come to make it work. I have come to write it into your life, and transfer it into your experience.'

It is this alone that makes the Gospel make sense, and is so utterly exciting! It meets our need exactly where it lies. We shall explore it in the next chapter.

8: Turning Commandments Into Promises

We have looked in the previous chapter at the *purpose of the law*, and the *effect of the law*. The purpose of the law is to reveal the character of God. The effect of the law is to reveal the failure of man. None of that so far provides us with any solution to our need. It may be of academic interest to know, but it is in itself of no practical consequence, other than to create an awareness of guilt. Hence the law has always left people helpless. No one has ever been justified by the law. (Galatians 2:16) It may have made people aware of their sin but it has never saved anyone from their sin.

The highest function of the law is that it has been, 'put in charge to lead us to Christ'. (Galatians 3:24) That is why we must now come to the Lord Jesus Christ whose relationship to the law is to *fulfil the law*. 'I have not come to abolish the law, but to fulfil them.' (Matthew 5:17) The big question is: What does he mean?

He is not speaking of a vicarious fulfilling of the law on our behalf, though that is certainly true in regard to the ceremonial laws of the old covenant. In addition to the *moral law*, the ten commandments, God also gave *ceremonial law* to Israel, which involved rituals and regulations whereby a person could approach God. They were centred on the tabernacle, later the temple, and were mediated through the priesthood whose functions largely involved the presenting of sacrifices and offerings. In a very real sense the Lord Jesus fulfilled that law and, in so doing, abolished it. At the moment of Jesus' death outside Jerusalem, the curtain in the temple which divided the Most Holy Place from the Holy Place was torn from top to bottom. This was a divine act. It was not torn from bottom to top by a man, but top to bottom, out of man's reach. God tore the curtain, for when the Lord Jesus Christ 'became sin for us', and purchased our salvation by his own blood, the regulations of the old covenant were rendered null and void. Never again would God require the blood of a bull, a goat or a lamb. The priesthood was now defunct, the temple redundant and the law abolished. In this particular and limited sense, the Lord Jesus fulfilled and abolished the law.

However, in regard to the moral law, he has declared its permanency: 'Until heaven and earth disappear, not the smallest letter, nor the least stroke of a pen, will by any means disappear from the law.' (Matthew 5:18) He states the law to be more sure than the earth on which we stand, and even more sure than the heaven we anticipate! The law will outlive both of these, for as we have seen, the law is a revelation of the character of God and God does not change. He always has and always will be the same. His law will be as consistent as his character which it expresses.

What then does Jesus mean when he declares he will 'fulfil' it? I believe the answer to this question is vital to a proper understanding of his work as our Saviour. I will go further, and say that to understand this will unlock so much of the work of Christ that may otherwise be hazy in our thinking, and bring a new liberty and power to our experience.

Restoring The Glory Of God

To change the language without changing the meaning,

instead of asking, 'How is the law of God going to be fulfilled,' we could equally ask the question, 'How is the glory of God going to be restored?' You will recall that the law of God and the glory of God represent the same thing, they represent the character of God.

Therefore to fulfil the law of God is to restore the glory of God, which is to display the character of God. But how is the Lord Jesus to do this?

I will turn you to three Scriptures in three different parts of the Bible, and then link them together as an explanation of this statement of Jesus.

The first is in Colossians, where Paul speaking of his ministry writes: 'I have become its servant (of the church), by the commission God gave me to present to you the word of God in its fullness – the mystery that has been kept hidden for ages and generations, but is now disclosed to the saints.' Let us pause there a moment to get the full import of what is being said. Paul declares himself to be preaching the word of God 'in its fullness'. There is nothing omitted and nothing new that can be added. This is the full gospel, and it involves what Paul calls a 'mystery, kept hidden for ages and generations'.

In other words, up until now there has always been something that did not add up to a complete picture. There has always been a gap in the revelation. Something has been missing. When a prophet finished his prophesying he would go back to his home, sit down and scratch his head and say, 'That is all very well, but something important is missing from this.' When Moses received the law on Mount Sinai, he too will have gone back to his tent, sat down and scratched his head and said, 'Something is missing from the revelation. There has got to be more than this. A vital piece has been left out.'

It is this vital piece, the 'mystery' that will make the whole revelation of God complete, that Paul is about to declare. 'To them God has chosen to make known among

101

the Gentiles the glorious riches of this mystery, which is Christ in you, the hope of glory.' (Colossians 1:25–27) Let me remind you that 'glory' does not mean heaven! The glory of God is the character of God. We have sinned and come short of the glory of God, and now, Christ living in us is our hope of hitting the target that we have only ever missed by our own resources. John had declared that when the Word became flesh, we 'saw his glory, the glory of the One and Only who came from the Father full of grace and truth', but the very quality of life once seen in Jesus, he now imparts to us by his indwelling presence.

We have missed the target of the glory of God. This has been the measure of our sin. Now, with Christ living his life within us, He is our hope of hitting the target, and displaying once again the 'glory of God'.

The Law In Our Hearts

God spoke to Jeremiah about the new covenant he was going to establish with his people in these terms: ' "This is the covenant I will make with the house of Israel after that time," declares the Lord. I will put my law in their minds and write it on their hearts. I will be their God, and they will be my people.' (Jeremiah 31:33) The new covenant will not involve a *rewriting* of the law for it represents the character of God which is absolute. It will involve a *relocating* of the law. The law that was then engraved on tablets of stone, and kept in the ark of the covenant in the Most Holy Place in the temple in Jerusalem, was going to be engraved in people's minds and written in people's hearts – whatever that may mean, and we shall see shortly! The point we make at this stage is that the law itself will be the very substance of the new covenant, but written in the minds and hearts of people.

Later God spoke to Ezekiel about the new covenant: 'And I will put my Spirit in you and move you to follow my decrees and be careful to keep my laws.' (Ezekiel 36:27) The declaration that God will place his Spirit in people was going to be something new. In the Old Testament the Holy Spirit was sometimes 'upon' people, occasionally he 'filled' people and a few times he is described as being 'in' people, but usually he was only 'with' people. If we want a general statement about the work of the Holy Spirit with people before and after Pentecost, then Jesus gave it to his disciples in the Upper Room discourse on the week he died when he said of the Spirit: 'He lives *with you* and will be *in you*.' (John 14:17) Generally speaking, in the pre-pentecost era the Spirit was *with* people. Now God tells Ezekiel that under the new covenant the Spirit is going to reside *in* people, and the end result is that he will 'move you to follow my decrees and keep my laws'. The consequence of the Spirit indwelling human lives is that they will keep the law of God.

If we tie these three statements together, we get an explanation of what it means for Jesus to fulfil the law. I will do so after recapitulating on the basic problem of mankind, against the background of which we will understand the solution of Jesus. Here are five propositions:

1 God made man in his image. In the moral behaviour of man was to be seen the moral behaviour of God.
2 Man sinned and came short of the glory of God. He no longer showed what God is like.
3 The law was given to reveal the character of God which is the glory of God, so that man in seeing what God is like, may see what he is supposed to be like.
4 The law only exposed man's inability and left him hopelessly condemned.
5 Christ came to fulfil the law. By the indwelling presence of his Spirit in man, he will write the law

on their minds, place it in their hearts, and be their hope of the glory of God. He will restore the moral character of God to the life of man.

This is the gospel! Man's need is not that he is guilty and needs to be forgiven. That is perfectly true, but is only the symptom of the real need. It is not simply that he is bound for hell and needs to be bound for heaven. That is also true, but is the consequence of his salvation or lack of it, not the substance of it. Man's need is that he is godless and needs to be made Godly. He is detached from the indwelling presence of God and needs to be reconciled to God.

The Command Becomes A Promise

This is what Jesus meant by coming to 'fulfil the law'. What has been a command under the old covenant is going to be a promise under the new covenant!

I can best illustrate this by a story I heard of a man who was converted to Christ whilst serving a prison sentence. He was in prison for stealing. During this time, someone had come and introduced him to Christ and he was born again of the Holy Spirit. On his release from prison the first thing he wanted to do was visit a church. Not knowing which to attend, he picked one at random on his first Sunday morning of release and sat on the back row. He looked up to the front, and to his dismay, located on two plaques either side of the pulpit were written the ten commandments. There were five down one side, and five down the other. He thought to himself: 'That is the last thing I want to see. I know my weakness. I know my failure. The last thing I want to do is sit here and read those laws that only condemn me.' But he did read them, and as he did so he realized he was reading them very differently.

Previously he had read 'You shall not steal' and it was a command! This time it read 'You shall not steal' and it was a promise, as a father might say to a child he is holding 'You will not fall'. It is not a command of the father to the child, but his promise to the child. It is he who will prevent the fall. He responded to God: 'Thank you Lord, but why?' 'Because I have put my Spirit in you, and will move you to follow my decrees and keep my laws.'

Previously he had read 'You shall not bear false witness.' It was a command. Now it read, 'You shall not bear false witness' and it was a promise. 'Thank you Lord,' he responded, 'Why?' 'Because I have put my law in your mind and written it on your heart, and you need not bear false witness.'

Previously he had read 'You shall not commit adultery' and it was a command. Now he read 'You shall not commit adultery' and it was a promise! 'Thank you Lord,' he responded, 'Why?' 'Because Christ in you is your hope of hitting the target you have previously fallen short of: the glory of God.'

Previously he had read 'You shall not covet.' It had been a command. Now he read 'You shall not covet' and it was a promise! 'Thank you Lord. Why?' he responded again. 'Because I have not come to abolish the law. I have come to fulfil it, to make it work.'

Isn't that wonderful? The very law that had only ever condemned him had become a promise that liberated him. This of course is the gospel! It is not simply the means of getting us into heaven by the skin of our teeth, but of restoring to us what was lost in the Fall, the life of God, and that is what qualifies us for heaven. What was commanded under the old covenant, and established on Sinai, has been promised under the new covenant, established at Calvary and implemented at Pentecost.

This is the meaning behind the oft debated statement of Paul: 'Sin will not be your master, because you are not under law but under grace.' (Romans 6:14) I have participated in long discussions over the intention of that verse, most of which have completely missed the point! The meaning is really very simple. The Greek word translated 'grace' is the word 'charis'. It means 'gift'. The word has found its way into the English vocabulary. We speak of people having 'charisma', by which we mean they are 'gifted'. When Paul states that 'Sin will not be your master because you are not under law but under grace,' he is saying that what was a command given to Moses, has become a gift given by Jesus, and consequently, 'sin will not be your master!' As the forgiveness of sins is a gift, so the deliverance from sin is a gift. As justification is a gift, so sanctification is a gift.

What The Law Could Not Do, God Did

The demands of the law have not changed, but resources that equal the demands of the law have now been made available. 'What the law was powerless to do in that it was weakened by the sinful nature, God did by sending his own Son in the likeness of sinful man...in order that the righteous requirements of the law might be fully met in us, who do not live according to the sinful nature but according to the Spirit.' (Romans 8:3–4) Paul is stating that the end product of the Gospel is that the 'righteous requirements of the law might be fully met in us', so that when the law says, 'You shall not steal,' we have the potential not to anymore. Not that we are more disciplined than previously, but that Jesus Christ lives in us, and he never steals, so we need never steal. When the law says, 'You shall not bear false witness,' we don't need to anymore. Not because we are trying harder, but because Jesus Christ lives in us, and he does not lie. When the law says 'You shall not covet,' we don't, not because we are trying hard not to, but Jesus Christ lives in us, and he is

106

not greedy and does not covet. The Christian life is not a consequence of what I do for God, but a consequence of what he does in me.

Jesus once declared: 'By this shall all men know that you are my disciples if you love one another.' (John 13:35) Why did Jesus state love to be the evidence of genuine Christian discipleship? The reason is straightforward. Scripture elsewhere states 'God is love' (1 John 4:16) and the evidence that we belong to him is that when people meet us they see him! His character is demonstrated in our behaviour. That is why the 'fruit of the spirit' is the character of Christ. (*See* Galatians 5:22–23) It is not obtainable by imitating Christ, but only by allowing Christ to be himself in us.

From One Degree Of Glory To Another

From what we have seen above, it might seem logical to conclude that the end product of true Christianity is that we become perfect, or that at least, this is our potential. But that would be a mistaken conclusion.

Paul writes: 'And we who with unveiled faces all reflect the Lord's glory are being transformed into his likeness with ever increasing glory which comes from the Lord who is the Spirit.' (2 Corinthians 3:38) Notice the tense Paul uses. He does not say we '*have been* transformed into his likeness' in the completed past, nor does he say '*we shall be* transformed into his likeness' in the future yet to be experienced, but we '*are being* transformed' in the present continuous tense. It is a process at work now, though yet to be completed in the future. We are on a journey, the destiny of which is perfection as God is perfect. In this life, our growth is 'from one degree of glory to another' until we meet him face to face. Then we will be glorified!

This is the measure of our spiritual growth. Spiritual growth is not measured by the amount of Scripture I may have memorised, or the amount of time I spend alone in Bible-reading and prayer, or in the amount of Christian service in which I engage, or the number of people I lead to Christ. All of that is valuable and good. But the true quality of spiritual growth is measured by the extent to which the character of Jesus Christ is more readily and more easily seen in me today than he used to be.

In practical terms, growth in godliness will be seen in the way a man treats his wife, in the way parents handle and treat their children, giving to them the right to grow up in a home where they may look to their mother and father to get some idea of what God is like. The way we go about our work, drive our cars, spend our money, talk to our neighbours, talk about our neighbours, do our work and pay our bills will all begin to reflect the character of God. The end product of our salvation is not that we go to heaven when we die (though we certainly will) but that the indwelling life of Jesus by his Holy Spirit is reproducing the character of God in us, so that people in our company, may get some glimpse of what he is like.

We are being changed from 'one degree of glory to another' into his image. Until one day we will discover fully that 'those he justified he also glorified.' (Romans 8:30) To be glorified simply means we will be fully restored to that image in which God first made man in the Garden of Eden. That will not take place until we have arrived in heaven. Then, if I bump into you on those pearly streets, I may be forgiven for thinking at first that you were Jesus! Won't that be wonderful? Not that we will all be physical replicas, for I am sure we will not. We will not be clones of Jesus, we will be individuals as much as we are now, but in our moral perfection, we shall be as he is.

In the meantime, this is our goal, and the end product to which the Holy Spirit relentlessly carries us, as we live in humble submission to him as our Lord and His Spirit as our Life.

Only Christ Can Live The Christian Life

Some years ago I was conducting a week of Bible-teaching meetings in a church in the East of England. On the last night I wanted to shake hands with a few people and thank them for attending. There was a nineteen-year-old boy there who had attended every night. He sat just a few rows back, and was clearly in earnest as he listened attentively to everything I said. I went across to him that evening, thanked him for being there, and told him I had been encouraged by his obvious appetite for the things of God. I then looked him in the eye and asked: 'Are you a Christian?'. I had for several days sensed that perhaps he wasn't. Without any hesitation he looked straight back at me and replied: 'No, I am not.' 'Would you like to become one?' I asked. He told me that every night of the week he had gone home wishing he could become a Christian, 'but I have a problem.'

'What is that?' I enquired.

'I know myself too well,' he replied, 'and I know that if I became a Christian tonight, by Monday morning I would not be able to keep it up. I know what I am like. I know my weaknesses, and rather than become a Christian now and make a mess of it, I would prefer to wait until I was more sure of keeping it up.'

I told him I was sure God was delighted with his integrity and honesty, and that he was actually correct, and if he did become a Christian that night he would not be able to keep it up!

'Then what is the point?' was his logical question.

'What have I been talking about this week?' I asked. 'Have I been giving you techniques for spiritual growth? Have I given you ten methods of reaching maturity, or three steps to making the Christian life work?'

'No,' he responded, 'you haven't.'

'Then what have I been talking about?'

109

'Every night you have ended up talking about Jesus Christ.'

'You are exactly right,' I replied. 'The whole point of the Christian life is that only Jesus Christ can live it. It is not a technique or a discipline but a relationship where you allow Jesus Christ to make his home in your heart and allow him to live in you the life you could never live by yourself. If you could live it by yourself then why bother becoming a Christian, just go and do it! But of course you can't, which is why Jesus Christ is indispensable, not just as the One who forgives you of your past, but as the One who comes to live within you and replaces your life with his.'

After explaining this for a little while, he suddenly said to me: 'Isn't that fantastic. I have never seen that before!' I wasn't very encouraged by that for I had preached it every night of the week and he had taken a book full of notes! You can hear something again and again, you can learn the language, and assume you know its truth, but it is all clouded in mist until suddenly the light goes on, and the truth comes alive. It is the moment of revelation that must always accompany the preaching of truth if it is to be effective. This was his moment of revelation. He saw it all, and that night he gave his life to Christ and was born again of the Holy Spirit.

About nine months later, that particular church planned a weekend together in a conference centre near their town. They invited me to join them and give some Bible teaching, and I was free and able to do so. On my way to the centre the weather changed and began to snow, which slowed me down so that I arrived much later than planned. Someone met me at the door, told me they had been in their first session for thirty minutes waiting for me to arrive, and would I go and give my first message straight away!

When I got into the conference hall, who should be

110

leading the singing but my friend. He introduced me and I spoke to the group. When I had finished I went across to him and said I had not expected to see him there.

'Why not?' he asked.

'Because I did not think you would be able to keep up the Christian life.'

'Of course I can't keep it up,' he said. 'If I could, I wouldn't need Christ! The whole point of the Christian life is that Jesus Christ comes to live in us the life that we ourselves cannot live . . .'

I interrupted him, 'All right, I have heard it all before. But does it work?'

'Well I am still here!' he said.

That night he introduced me to his twin sister. I did not realise he had a twin, and when I met her I sensed immediately that she was a Christian. The following afternoon we were in conversation together and I asked her how long she had known the Lord. 'About four months now,' she replied.

I asked her how that had happened, and she told me a very interesting story. About nine months ago she had noticed her brother change. They had been close all of their lives and knew each other intimately, but he was suddenly quite different. One day she asked him if he thought he had changed at all.

'I wish I had,' he replied to her, 'but I don't think I have.'

'Why do you wish you had?' she asked.

'Because I became a Christian recently, and I thought I might change, but nothing seems to have happened.'

'I can see all kinds of changes,' she assured him.

'Can you really?' he asked.

Let me pause there a moment. I find that very encouraging. The last person who will see clearly what is going on in your life is you! I have very little time for introspection or spiritual naval gazing! When I look inside myself I see an old nature at war with the spirit, looking for opportunity to sin. The old me is utterly corrupt and condemned. We will be conscious of the battle, but the wonderful thing is that it may be other people who see the victory of Jesus long before I have any inkling of it myself. That is why our instruction is to 'fix your eyes on Jesus, the author and finisher of our faith,' (Hebrews 12:2) and not upon ourselves.

The Glory Is Seen Outside The Camp

For the children of Israel in the desert, the manifestation of the glory of God was always outside the camp. Have you noticed that? When you look into your heart you see its corruption. When others look at you from outside they may see the glory! It will be true in your church and in almost any Christian ministry in which you will engage. From the inside you will see the 'flesh warring with the Spirit', and you may be tempted to be discouraged by the battle. But if God is in it, people outside will be seeing the glory of God! You may wonder how he uses a church like yours, or a ministry like the one you know well, or people like you whose heart you know to wander so easily. But he will! When Moses came down Mount Sinai with the law of God in his hands, 'he was not aware that his face was radiant.' (Exodus 34:29) The law Moses carried in his hands was expressed by the glory of God in his face, but he was the only one who did not know it! 'The Israelites could not look steadily at the face of Moses because of its glory.' (2 Corinthians 3:7) Moses himself, in his anger at finding the people worshipping a golden calf, had smashed the two tablets of stone on the ground, and had probably felt guilty and miserable as a result. Yet despite what Moses knew about his heart, the people saw the glory of God. They will see him in you too, but you won't! You are too close. The glory will be visible outside the camp, even when you least sense it! That will be God's doing so take no credit.

This was true of my friend. His sister told me: 'I watched him for five months, and at the end of that time I asked him to show me how I could have what he had, and he led me to Christ.' I bumped into that fellow once or twice since. Each time he was enjoying the Lord Jesus Christ as his life. He discovered the day he became a Christian, something I did not discover for several years. Only Jesus Christ can live the Christian life. The whole point of the Gospel is that Jesus Himself comes to live in us the life we can never live by ourselves.

God made you in his image. He gave the law to reveal what that image is. The law only exposed your failure and left you condemned. Jesus came to cleanse you of your guilt, so that he might then come and live his life in your body. Only then can he fulfil the law. Only then can you be the person you were created to be and find the fulfilment destined for you from the creation of the world. Have you discovered that yet?

9: The Way In To The Action

We have looked at the contents of the ark, and before moving on, will take a moment to review and summarize what we have said so far. The ark of the covenant has represented for us the Lord Jesus Christ. It was the presence of God among the nation of Israel, the place where they were to meet with God, and the place from which he would speak to them.

The ark was located in the Most Holy Place in the tabernacle, later to be replaced by the temple. This was God's 'home', the place where he resided and the place where he was approached. All of this was designed by God as a 'shadow of the good things that are coming – not the realities themselves'. (Hebrews 10:1) The realities which this foreshadowed came in Christ. The temple as a brick and mortar structure where the presence of God was to be found, has been abolished from God's programme. God lives in a new home, he lives in the lives of his people. Paul wrote: 'Do you not know that your body is a temple of the Holy Spirit, who is in you, whom you have received from God? You are not your own; you were bought at a price.' (1 Corinthians 6:19–20)

We have also seen that the contents of the ark, represent the nature of true spiritual experience as they portray what we have received in the Lord Jesus Christ. As the down payment of God's gift to us, the presence and 'sealing' of the Holy Spirit is the deposit of God, assuring us of what is to come, for he has 'set his seal of ownership on us, and put his Spirit in our hearts as a deposit, guaranteeing what is to come'. (2 Corinthians 1:22) Having entered our lives and sealed the covenant of our relationship at new birth, his purpose is to lead us on into fullness and fruitfulness. This reality has been portrayed in God's gift of *manna* to his people. Having delivered them from their years of slavery and bondage in Egypt, he sustained them in the desert, with food that tasted of the real thing, for it 'tasted of honey', but it did not satisfy them, for he did not plan to satisfy them outside of Canaan, the land 'flowing with milk and honey'.

The supernatural life in *Aaron's staff that budded*, which blossomed and produced almonds, portrays the supernatural life of God in every Christian. It is only as we live in obedience to his instructions and rely upon his power that we will see his life expressed in real fruitfulness. 'I chose you and appointed you to go and bear fruit — fruit that will last.' (John 15:16)

Finally, in the revelation of the law on the *two tablets of stone*, God demonstrated his own character as the moral image in which he had created man. The law exposes our inability, but the end product of the work of Christ is that he fulfils the law in our own experience, and restores to us the godliness we were originally created to express.

This encompasses the full orb of God's dealings with man. The manna typifies the *presence of God* in every true Christian. Aaron's staff that budded demonstrates the *power of God* which is to be at work through every true Christian. The law reveals *the purpose of God* that he has determined for every true Christian.

Strictly According To Pattern

There is an important question concerning all of this which we need to think about at this stage: How do I enter into the good of this provision in Christ? How do I gain access to the Most Holy Place in which the ark was kept, and so enjoy the full provision of the Lord Jesus Christ for me? So often we learn to be content with a low level of spiritual life, not because we choose it to be that way, but because we do not know how it may be different.

Once again it is in the shadows of the old covenant we find hidden the realities of the new. Access to God then, foreshadowed the means of access to God now. Although we are given 'confidence to enter the Most Holy Place by the blood of Jesus' (Hebrews 10:19) we enter it not glibly or cheaply, but through a predetermined pattern that God gave Moses on Sinai. When God revealed to Moses the tabernacle details, he strictly charged him, 'See that you make them according to the pattern shown you on the mountain.' (Exodus 25:40) The pattern is now obsolete, but the principles expressed still stand as the means by which we may know and experience God.

There were five barriers to the Most Holy Place in which was located the ark of the presence of God. It would be inappropriate to examine them in fine detail now, for we are concerned with the principles rather than the details. We will however, survey the procedure, enshrined in the regulations God gave to Moses concerning the tabernacle. This will teach us the timeless means of unhindered access to God, and the consequent enjoyment of all his provision for us.

1. The Altar Of Burnt Offering

You will recall that the tabernacle was a rectangular tent, forty-five feet in length, and fifteen feet wide. It was located in an enclosed courtyard that was one-hundred-and-fifty feet long and seventy-five feet wide. When approaching the tabernacle through the entrance on the east side, the first and most visible feature in the courtyard surrounding the tabernacle was an altar, about four-and-a-half feet high, and about seven-and-a-half feet wide and long. It was here that sacrifices and offerings were made to God on a fire that never went out. There were two purposes.

Firstly, there were the burnt, guilt sin and fellowship offerings that atoned for sin. These were required by God and were mandatory. Through the shedding of blood, sin was covered and the guilty set free. We discussed earlier in the book the limitations of animal blood, but for now, there is one point that stands clear. Access to God begins with the shedding of blood, the laying down of life in substitutionary payment for the penalty of sin. This alone, is the starting point. The altar points us to the cross of the Lord Jesus Christ, the indispensable starting point to any fellowship with God. We must not fail to understand three aspects of the cross if we are to fully appropriate its benefits.

It was *substitutionary*. It was my death Christ died and my penalty he incurred. Therefore though I stand responsible and guilty of my sin, I owe God nothing for it. Jesus paid it in full! As a consequence of my repentance towards God and my faith in Jesus Christ, I become indwelt by his Holy Spirit and am brought into union with Christ which involves union in his death. Paul wrote: 'We have been united with him in his death . . . for our old self was crucified with him.' (Romans 6:5–6) In Christ, God saw me die in union with him, the penalty of my sin fully dealt with. I may be a debtor to God's mercy, for his love alone initiated salvation, but I am not a debtor to his justice, for God's just demand for punishment has been fully and finally met. His justice has been satisfied, for in Christ I died, and God sees me in him.

It is *satisfactory*. God requires nothing more. That is why penance of any kind is unnecessary. Any need to take further punishment, to pay a fine, to run around the block ten times or to be given only a conditional discharge, whereby he forgives me now but will punish me later if I do the same thing again, immediately undermines the quality of his death and the value of his blood.

It is *sufficient*. There is no depth of depravity for which the blood of Jesus has not atoned. No one is in an unforgivable state, and no sin can be committed so many times that we become irredeemable, and to believe so would be to blaspheme the cross.* To doubt the possibility of complete and total forgiveness is to deny the effectiveness of the cross.

Without the confidence that we stand justified before God on the basis of the death of Christ alone, we can neither know God nor enjoy his presence. This is the starting point. To ignore or bypass the cross as indispensable on my behalf, is to trip on 'a stone that causes men to stumble and a rock that makes them fall.' (1 Peter 2:8) Have you been to the cross, to the altar where the fire never burns out, and is always available to liberate you from your sin and justify you before God?

Secondly, there were offerings made at the altar that did not involve blood. The grain offering was to be brought voluntarily. This represents the offering of the person himself, his body and possessions. These were generally presented along with some animal sacrifice in order to show the connection between forgiveness for sin and the full consecration of the person to God.

In the cross of Christ two things took place, both of which must be made real in our experience. Firstly, *Christ*

---

*Blasphemy against the Holy Spirit (e.g. Matthew 12:31, Mark 3:28, Luke 12:10) is to resist the Holy Spirit's conviction and revelation of sin, so as to refuse the only possible means of forgiveness. Hence to blaspheme against the Holy Spirit is spoken of by Jesus as being 'guilty of an eternal sin', for to not respond to his conviction is to close all possibilities. There is no alternative means than this for forgiveness.

died for us. Secondly, *we died with Christ.* We not only thank him for his blood poured out on our behalf, but we identify ourselves as 'crucified with Christ' (Galatians 2:20) as a present status.

This is not something I *do* but must recognize as *done*. As I now consider there to be no value in my *sins*, I must also consider there to be no value in my *self*. All that derives from myself, the old natural me, is as condemned as my sin is condemned, for 'I know that nothing good lives in me, that is in my sinful nature,' (Romans 7:18) which should literally read 'in my flesh'. Paul's use of the word 'flesh' (that some more recent translations have been unable to cope with) refers not to the physical body, but to all that a person is in himself, apart from God. Anything and everything that has its origin in *me* as opposed to having its origin in *God* is 'of the flesh', and the flesh cannot please God. It is good only for crucifixion. Anything I may do for God, is the working of the flesh. Anything God does for me, is the working of the Spirit. The reason I am to recognize myself as crucified with Christ is because not only is Jesus my substitute in death, but he is my substitute in life, 'Nevertheless I live, yet not I but Christ lives in me.' He died my death, he now lives as my life. For that to be possible as a daily reality, I must place all that is of self on the altar of God until it is reduced to ashes. Then, I may find my fullness in Christ.

This was the twofold function of the altar inside the entrance to the tabernacle courts. The blood offerings to deal with *sin*. The grain offerings to deal with *self*. It was at this altar that any approach to fellowship with God began. Until we avail ourselves of the full measure of the cross, in both of its dimensions, we shall not experience the fullness of God's purposes for us and in us.

2. The Bronze Basin

Between the altar and the entrance to the tabernacle itself was a bronze basin, which held water for washing. This was exclusively for the use of the priests, who washed their hands and their feet before entering the tabernacle itself, and before handling the utensils at the altar for burnt offerings.

The terms required for entering the presence of God and for handling the things of God is cleanliness. 'Who may ascend the hill of the Lord? Who may stand in his holy place?' asks David, and then he gives his answer: 'He who has clean hands and a pure heart, who does not lift up his soul to an idol or swear by what is false.' (Psalm 24:3–4) A person is justified when they come to the cross in repentance and faith. That never needs repetition. It is a completed act and has become their standing before God. God has imputed to them his righteousness, and 'there is now no condemnation for those who are in Christ Jesus.' (Romans 8:2) However, there is an ongoing need for cleansing.

I think this is best illustrated when Jesus took a basin in the Upper Room with his disciples, and began to wash their feet. Peter protested: 'You shall never wash my feet.' When Jesus insisted, Peter swung to the other extreme: ' "Then Lord, not just my feet but my hands and my head as well!" Jesus answered: "A person who has had a bath needs only to wash his feet; his whole body is clean." ' (John 13:6–10) The basin with which Jesus washed the feet of the disciples would seem to relate to the basin in the court of the tabernacle. The cross is our bath! There we are cleansed and justified. But we get our hands and our feet dirty! In the sinful environment in which we live, and with the sinful flesh which battles in our hearts, we fall and we sin. We do not need the bath of justification again, but we do need the basin of cleansing, again and again and again. 'If we confess our sins, he is faithful and just and will forgive us our sins and purify us from all unrighteousness.' (1 John 1:9) As the Levites washed their hands and feet at the bronze basin, before daring to touch the utensils of the altar, or daring to enter the tabernacle itself, so we need constantly to come for cleansing or we shall be obstructed in our walk with God and service for him.

I find the materials used to make the basin very interesting. 'They made the bronze basin and its bronze stand from the mirrors of the women who served at the entrance to the Tent of Meeting.' (Exodus 38:8) The utensils originally manufactured for the purpose of turning attention in on themselves, were instead converted to an instrument for turning attention on God. If we become introspective about our spiritual lives we are almost certain to get discouraged, disappointed and even despairing. Turn any mirror on Christ, for our cleanliness and righteousness is to be found only in him. Keep the attention on his generosity, his mercy and his love and in keeping him in our focus we will find our own true significance.

3. The Table Of Bread

Having passed by the altar and the basin, we enter from the courtyard in to the tabernacle itself. In the first section, the Holy Place, were three pieces of furniture, which had to be passed by before access to the inner room, containing the ark of the covenant, could be possible.

On the north side, to the right when entering, was a table on which was placed the 'bread of the presence'. These were twelve loaves in two rows of six, freshly renewed every Sabbath day. Aaron and his sons were to eat the loaves, as part of the ritual of the offerings. Here they would find sustenance and strength.

God has more to do for us than justify us by the blood of Christ, and then keep us clean. We need strengthening and sustaining. The bread is described as the 'bread of his presence'. It is he himself who is our strength. It is Christ who declared: 'I am the bread of life. He who comes to me will never go hungry.' (John 6:35) It is not fellowship with other Christians, it is not good teaching, it is not doctrine, it is not great experiences, it is not even the Bible that is the bread that sustains, strengthens and satisfies us. It is Christ alone. These other things are important and necessary as they bring us to Christ, and become a means of bringing him to us, but they can never be his substitute. I may preach messages that people appreciate and even enjoy, but if I have not left them with Christ I have not fed them and I have not satisfied them, and will only perpetuate their spiritual immaturity and leave them hungry for something more.

This is the primary reason for which we are to read the Scriptures. It is through the written word that we discover the Living Word, for the supreme revelation of Christ is in the Bible. If you read the Bible for the primary purpose of getting to know the Bible it will have little true value in your life. It may make you biblically literate and doctrinally aware, but will leave you spiritually poor. If you read the Bible to get to know Christ, the Scriptures will be a source of life, and will thrill you, feed you, excite you and satisfy you! But you must go through the written word to the Living word every time.

4. The Golden Lampstand

Opposite the table of bread, on the south side of the Holy Place was a seven-pronged lampstand. It was trimmed and lit every evening and through the long hours of the night it threw back the darkness and gave light. The source of the light was pure olive oil, freshly pressed, which had to be renewed every day. Not only did it have immediate benefit in the light it gave, but the Lord said to Moses about the lamp: 'This is to be a lasting ordinance for the generations to come.' (Leviticus 24:3) There is a message here designed for all time!

This can only but be a picture of the Holy Spirit. Oil is a consistent symbol of the Spirit right through the Bible, and it is the Spirit who illuminates, it is he who gives us direction and he who gives guidance. It is in the Spirit we need to be renewed every day. Jesus said to his disciples, 'You are the light of the world'. (Matthew 5:16) It is the Christian who will be God's lampstand, and in whom will be seen the light of God. Jesus said: 'I am the light of the world. Whoever follows me will never walk in darkness but will have the light of life.' (John 8:12) This is part of the privilege of the Christian life, that we live in the light, and that we beam the light in to the dark world. But lampstands need an energy source! True as it is that we are to be lights, there can be no light without oil! The lampstand is merely the vehicle through which the oil can express its capacity and release its energy. The lamp has no capability of its own, and is not the source of the light. It is the Holy Spirit, the dynamic of God, whose life and energy is expressed through God's people.

We are the lampstand, and as such we may be the direction to which people look, and the one's from whom they receive light, but the source of that light is the Spirit of God, upon whom we must remain totally dependent. He is to fill our lives and express his own power and beauty through us.

Paul's command is to 'Be very careful then how you live – not as unwise, but as wise . . . do not be foolish, but understand what the Lord's will is . . . Be filled with the Spirit.' (Ephesians 5:15–18). This is the will of God for every child of God. To not live in the fullness of his Spirit is to be foolish, as well as disobedient. The tense in which Paul literally writes this is the present continuous, 'Be *being* filled with the Spirit'. Like the lampstand in the tabernacle that needed renewing with oil every day, so we must not live on past experience of his filling, but keep in such relationship with him that 'inwardly we are being renewed every day.' (2 Corinthians 4:16).

There can hardly be a greater judgement of God on his people than that threatened in the letter of Jesus to the church in Ephesus. He said: 'If you do not repent, I will come to you and remove your lampstand from its place.' (Revelation 2:5) They had been grieving the Holy Spirit, and so quenching his role amongst them that the light, of which he was the source, was in danger of being put out.

When we quench the Spirit we drive God out, not in relation to our salvation but in relation to our usefulness and fruitfulness. The ability of the church in Ephesus to be what they were supposed to be was about to be snuffed out. They had neglected to renew the oil of the Holy Spirit as a daily discipline of life. It is only the oil that can make the lamp burn.

5. The Altar Of Incense

We now come to the final piece of furniture before the curtain which separated the Holy Place from the Most Holy Place and it is another altar, the altar of incense.

This was the place where fragrant incense was to be burned every morning. No other kind of incense was to be burned on this altar, and no burnt offering, grain offering or drink offering was ever to be offered here. Only once a year, on the Day of Atonement, as the High Priest made his way in to the Most Holy Place, was he to sprinkle blood from the sin offering on its horns.

The chief function of this altar, was to offer an aroma, and it was an aroma for God! God has a sense of smell!

As with all physical human references to God, this is an anthropomorphism. But we must ask the question — What aroma pleases God? To what do his senses respond with joy and delight? Paul writes: 'But thanks be to God, who . . . through us spreads everywhere the fragrance of the knowledge of him. For we are to God the aroma of Christ among those who are being saved and those who are perishing.' (2 Corinthians 2:14–15) Putting it bluntly and perhaps crudely, Paul says that we smell to God of Jesus!

What that means practically is perhaps clear from another statement in the Book of Revelation. When the angel opened the seals in heaven, 'the smoke of the incense, together with the prayers of the saints, went up before God from the angel's hand.' (Revelation 8:4) If we are the aroma of Christ to God, and the prayers of the saints ascend to him as the smell of incense, then combining these two, I suggest that it is our fellowship with the Lord Jesus Christ, our intimacy with him, our knowledge of him, our communion with him that derives from prayer, which brings the pleasure of a sweet aroma to God.

If this is true, that through our union with Christ, brought about and made real by having been to the altar of burnt offering, to the bronze bowl for washing, to the table of the bread of his presence, and the lampstand burning with pure olive oil, then the goal to which all this has been leading, and which brings joy to the heart of God, is that we know and love his Son, and are in real living fellowship with him. To know the Bible, to know doctrine, to know the church, to know Christian service but to not have a growing and deepening knowledge of Christ himself, will all be ultimately futile, and as the 'wood, hay and straw' (1 Corinthians 3:11) on the Day of Judgement, be good only for destruction.

Here lies the crux of the matter. The Lord Jesus Christ is our friend, our saviour, our Lord and our Life. We know him, and we are known by him. We love him, and we are

125

loved by him. We trust him. We obey him. We want to please him. We worship him.

All divine truth will ultimately lead to this. All spiritual reality will ultimately derive from this.

Once a year on the Day of Atonement the altar of fragrant incense became soaked with the blood of the sin offering as Aaron poured it on the horns of the altar. That day the smell of burning blood mingled with the fragrance of the incense, brought a different smell to God.

On Calvary, the Lord Jesus Christ brought the ritual to fulfilment. As he, the aroma that delights God, was made to be sin, and mingled his sinless life with the sin of the world, he cried out: 'My God, my God, why have you forsaken me?' (Matthew 27:46) The tarnishing of the purity of Christ when the sins of the world were heaped upon him and he was made to 'be sin for us' (2 Corinthians 5:17) brought to the Father an unpleasant aroma, and heaven remained silent. The Father withdrew from the Son.

But do you know a very wonderful thing? As Jesus cried out those words on the cross, and then dismissed his spirit, 'At that moment the curtain of the temple was torn in two from top to bottom.' (Matthew 27:51) The curtain that had divided the Most Holy Place from the rest of the temple was ripped apart as a divine act. God broke out!

God was no longer to be approached in a building, through rituals and offerings that needed constant repetition. He had broken loose from the temple and its inner chamber. He would now invade the lives of men, women, boys and girls in any place and at any time, if they would be willing to receive him. They now would become the temple of his Spirit, the place he would make his home, and the place he would do his work!

As the blood mingled with the fragrant incense on the altar before the curtain in the tabernacle, Aaron knew that at any moment now he would be given access into the Most

Holy Place where he would meet with God. The curtain would be opened and he would pass through. I wonder if he knew that one day the mingling of the blood of the sin offering with the beautiful aroma of the Son of God himself would not just open the curtain but rip it apart, never ever to be closed again, so that man need never ever be veiled again from his presence!

This is the ground of our confidence before God. We are not pulling at the curtain trying to force access. It was ripped from the top and it was ripped from the inside. God broke out, to now reside in any human heart who would receive him, and become the temple of his Holy Spirit.

Boldness To Enter In

Do you now see why we have 'boldness to enter the Most Holy Place'? This is not a boldness born of presumption, but a boldness born in humility, where we recognize there is nothing we can do, but enter in to what Christ has done. We cannot earn nor take credit for access to God, we can only come to him in the Lord Jesus Christ who said, 'I am the way and the truth and the life. No one comes to the Father except through me.' (John 14:6)

We do not doubt that we stand justified before God, and have cleansing of our sins. This is our experience in the courtyard of God's tabernacle, and it opens the door to us. Then with confidence we may enter and find the bread of his presence to sustain us, the oil of his Spirit to enable us, and the aroma of Christ to distinguish us. It is all available in Christ.

The path we have followed through the tabernacle was the route taken by Aaron and the priesthood on behalf of the people. The ordinary citizen did not come himself. The priest was his representative, and his action was vicarious. He performed it on their behalf.

We take the same path, for we come with the same need, but we have a better priest. 'Christ came as high priest . . . he went through the greater and more perfect tabernacle . . . he entered the Most Holy Place once for all, by his own blood.' (Hebrews 9:11–12) This does not need repetition by him, it needs only appropriation by us.

But one last thing. It may be you know all of these things. This journey has been almost tedious in its predictability. There is nothing new you did not already know. Yet, the reality is, the Most Holy Place still seems to you to be curtained off. The ark of the covenant containing those ingredients so vital to your well being and usefulness, do not seem to be part of your life. The presence of God is still only a taste, the power of God is so rarely evident in any way, and the purpose of God to restore you to his image seems little more than an idle dream. Why?

There were times when the offerings and sacrifices of the tabernacle did not please God. Even though the people came at the right times, they brought the right offerings, they followed the right pattern, and were handled by the right priests, yet the effect of it all hardly hit the ceiling of the tabernacle roof, only to drop dead on the ground again. The people went home exactly as they had come. The people were unmoved and God was unimpressed!

There are a number of instances of this, but perhaps the last book of the Old Testament is the most appropriate for us just to look at, for it ends the era of temple worship before we meet the Lord Jesus Christ on the pages of the New Testament. Here God gives a diagnosis of failed temple rituals even though ordained by himself, and a challenge to prove it different.

Diagnosis Of Failure

God says: 'Oh, that one of you would shut the temple

doors, so that you would not light useless fires on my altar!'
Malachi 1:10) They lit the fire and they offered the
sacrifices, but they were useless! It wasn't as though they
did not care about this, for 'You flood the Lord's altar
with tears. You weep and wail because he no longer pays
attention to your offerings or accepts them with pleasure
from your hand.' (Malachi 2:13) It may be you have felt
this in your own life. In the seeming barrenness of your
heart before God there have been tears of frustration and
grief. Like these people you have wailed almost in despair.
It could not be much worse if the doors of God's temple
were shut and you were barred from access.

I wonder if in reading these pages you find this to be
true? We have thought of the work of Christ, and although
it may be a familiar territory to you, it has lacked the reality
of a genuine and ongoing experience in your own life.

This was true for these people, but the reason was not
difficult to track down. 'When you bring blind animals
for sacrifice, is that not wrong? When you sacrifice
crippled or diseased animals, is that not wrong?' (Malachi
1:8) ' ''When you bring injured, crippled or diseased
animals and offer them as sacrifices, should I accept them
from your hands?'' says the Lord.' (Malachi 1:13) It would
be only a superficial explanation to say that in offering
crippled animals they were violating the command to 'not
bring anything with a defect . . . it must be without defect
or blemish to be acceptable.' (Leviticus 22:20–21) Wrong
as their behaviour clearly was, this was only the symptom
of their problem. It was not their actions in regard to
system, but their attitude to God himself that lay at the
root.

Their attitude to the ritual was the symptom of their
attitude to God. It was with God they needed to do
business. They wanted his blessings, but they had vested
interests of their own, and they tried to mesh the two
together. Yes, they did believe in the need to approach

God through the sacrificial system, but why give the best of the livestock when a blind bull, a crippled lamb, or a mangy old goat would suffice? With the acquiescence of the priests they fobbed God off by technically going through all the correct rituals – or so they thought. If they were to experience reality from God, he must receive honesty from them!

We may say our prayers, read our Bible, attend church, engage in service, and 'cling to the old rugged cross', but remain barren if these have in some way become a substitute for Christ himself. It is not the cross, but the Christ of the cross who saves us. It is not our prayers, but the God to whom we pray that hears us. It is not our service, but the power in which we do it that brings its fruit. It is not our church attendance, but the centrality of Christ that breathes reality and vitality.

What are you relying on as the source of your spiritual well-being, that is less than God himself? On an experience of God? Then forget it. On attending church? Then forget it. On creating certain feelings? Then forget it. On hours in prayer? Then forget it. On observing the sacraments? Then forget it. All of these are legitimate, good and will have their important function in our lives. But they are not the substance of spiritual life, they are only aides to it.

Challenge To Prove God

God issued a challenge through Malachi to prove him. To prove him is to have truth translated into genuine spiritual experience. Part of the symptom of the people having lost touch with reality and therefore desecrating the rituals, was that they did not pay their tithes. This was more than the giving of ten per cent of their income to God. The tithe was acknowledged in the covenant as already belonging to God: 'A tithe of everything from the land, whether grain from the soil or fruit from the trees, belongs to the Lord; it is holy to the Lord.' (Leviticus 27:30) It was not a donation to God, it was already his. To hold it back was to be guilty of robbing God.

In holding back the tithe, they did not give to God what belonged to God. They tried to get away with surrendering as little as possible, and were reaping the consequences of spiritual barrenness and poverty, despite their token fulfilment of the temple rituals.

God's final challenge to them, and his final challenge of the Old Testament, was to bring the tithe into the storehouse, to give God what is his, to acknowledge his demands upon them and see that they are done. ' "Test me in this," says the Lord Almighty, "and see if I will not throw open the floodgates of heaven and pour out so much blessing that you will not have room enough for it." ' (Malachi 3:10)

The challenge is straightforward. It is not to refine their beliefs, but simply to give God what was his, humbly and fully.

The promise is straightforward too! Instead of closing the doors of the temple which he had wished they would, he would open the floodgates of heaven and pour out so much they would not be able to contain it. Never again would they ever have less than enough!

God offers that challenge to you! Do you need to take him up on it? Perhaps you need to come to another altar where you may, 'offer your body as a living sacrifice, holy and pleasing to God — for this is your spiritual worship'. (Romans 12:1) Give God what belongs to him — yourself. You have been purchased by his blood. You are not doing him a favour, you are just giving what is his. As you do, he will open the floodgate of heaven upon you, and you will always have enough of what you need. This is his challenge and his invitation.

10: Temples Of The Living God

In the last chapter we followed the route in to the Most Holy Place, now opened for us by the Lord Jesus Christ. In opening it, he abolished it, for when the curtain of the temple tore from top to bottom on the day Jesus died, he rendered the building redundant! The temple of God is no longer made of bricks and mortar, located in Jerusalem. God now makes his home in the human heart, 'For we are the temple of the living God. As God has said, "I will live with them and walk among them, and I will be their God, and they will be my people." ' (2 Corinthians 6:16) This is where God lives, this is where he acts and this is where he displays his glory.

There is one more aspect we must look at. The ark of the covenant was located in the Most Holy Place of the temple. Following the Babylonian destruction of Jerusalem and the razing to the ground of the temple itself, the ark was either stolen or destroyed and has never been seen since. Fourteen years later the prophet Ezekiel had a vision of a new temple, and more details have been given to us of that than of Solomon's temple itself, even though Ezekiel's temple has never actually existed! We will not discuss the significance of the structure itself and whether it will literally be built one day (as some suppose), other than to conclude that to devote eight chapters of the Bible to describing it, must attribute to it some importance. For our present study, it gives us significant information about the kind of place God makes his home, and is therefore, to that extent, a description of his intention for his new temple, our bodies.

We will not follow Ezekiel through the guided tour of the outer court and various outer rooms on which he was taken; we shall go instead directly to the heart of the structure when 'The Spirit lifted me up and brought me into the inner court.' This was just outside the actual Holy Place and Most Holy Place. It was the area that surrounded it.

There Ezekiel saw, 'The glory of the Lord entered the temple . . . and the glory of the Lord filled the temple.' The glory of God we have already seen to be the presence and character of God, which he intended to be displayed in man when he created him in his own image. By nature we have 'sinned and come short of the glory of God', and no longer display his moral goodness. God's remedy has been to cleanse us of guilt, and place, 'Christ in you' as 'the hope of glory'. Now, indwelling us by his Spirit he will restore in us his own image and character that has been lost in the fall.

To be filled with the glory of God is to be so dominated by his Spirit so that all we say, do, and are, becomes a revelation of Jesus. This is God's ultimate goal in salvation. On meeting a true Christian we see again the glory and likeness of God.

But if all that seems idealistic and remote, a voice explains to Ezekiel why the temple radiates the glory of God: 'Son of man, this is the place of *my throne* and the place for *the soles of my feet*.' The display of the glory of God does not accidentally occur, but is a direct consequence of conditions that enable it to take place.

The Place Of My Throne

God states: 'This is the place of my throne.' In other words, 'This is the place where I am in charge and exercise my sovereignty and rule.' There will be no demonstration of the glory of God without a submission to the government of God. Submission to the Lordship of Jesus Christ in the heart of the Christian is not a 'super-de-lux' option, necessary for those who may want to take things a little further than the average Christian, but the fundamental disposition from which everything else derives. 'Christ died and returned to life so that he might be the Lord of both the dead and the living' (Romans 14:9) and therefore I must meet Christ not only as my redeemer and saviour but as Lord. These are his own terms and they are nonnegotiable. We will never live the Christian life effectively if we only see Christ as our servant. We must acknowledge and submit to him as our Master. It is true that he serves us, but it is never true that he is our servant. He is always our Master.

One of the simplest ways to trace the cause of spiritual breakdown in our lives, is to go back to the breakdown in obedience. I fear there is a danger in the church today to look for psychological and emotional causes to spiritual breakdown and barrenness, rather than volitional ones, where the will has been involved. We see ourselves as victims rather than perpetrators. We are the offended rather than the guilty. We are looking all the time for causes outside ourselves, rather than recognizing personal responsibility. There may be factors for which I am not to blame that have a direct bearing upon my own attitude and behaviour, and I may need help to resolve them, but consistently in Scripture God holds people responsible for themselves. God even told Samuel to stop sympathizing with Saul and pitying him, for he was reaping the consequences of his own making, for he did not obey God. (1 Samuel 16:1, cf 15:26) We have not been invited to bring a defence lawyer to the Judgement Seat of Christ, who will explain our circumstances, our environment, our background and even our families so that we may plead mitigating circumstances for our actions. No! Jesus Christ is totally capable of handling your life if you let him, and creating in you a godliness that has no explanation other than the miracle of God's working. But it must begin in humble submission at his throne.

That does not cover the whole story, for Ezekiel in his vision was to hear more. Not only is the temple of God, 'the place of my throne', but it is also 'the place of the souls of my feet'.

The Place Of The Soles Of My Feet

The *soles of my feet* is not an original expression. God said to Joshua when he entered Canaan, 'I will give you every place where you *set your foot*.' (Joshua 1:3) Later he reaffirmed: 'The land on which your feet have walked will be your inheritance.' (Joshua 14:9) God had said earlier of Caleb: 'I will give him and his descendants the land he *set his feet on*,' (Deuteronomy 1:26) and to the whole nation he promised, 'Every place where you *set your foot* will be yours.' (Deuteronomy 11:24) The setting of feet would occupy the land. It was to step into enemy territory and conquer it. The glory of God in the inner court of the temple was the consequence of conquered and occupied territory.

Paul writes of this same theme in the New Testament, when speaking of Jesus he says: 'For he must reign until he has put all his enemies *under his feet*. The last enemy to be destroyed is death. For he has put everything *under his feet*.' (1 Corinthians 15:25–26) To conquer an enemy is to put him under foot. We have already thought in an earlier chapter of the fact that the Lord Jesus Christ, by his resurrection from the dead, has faced the last enemy and defeated it, putting death itself under his feet.

That has fantastic implications! If Jesus has defeated the last enemy, then it means that every other enemy has been defeated too. If I have ten enemies and finally defeat the *last* one, it means the other nine are not still running around uncontrolled! If the *last* has been defeated, it means all other nine have been beaten too! Therefore, when Jesus Christ by his resurrection from the dead defeated the last enemy, he defeated every other enemy that may threaten to defeat me today! If I am being defeated today, I am being defeated by something which itself has been defeated by the resurrection of Christ from the dead.

This is why Paul can mock death as the ultimate enemy and write: 'Death has been swallowed up in victory. Where O death is your victory? Where O death is your sting?' (1 Corinthians 15:54–55) Death will still stalk us and we shall still die, but it will not defeat us. Sin will still stalk us and perfection in this life is not an option, but we need not be defeated, for in the cleansing of Jesus and the power of his indwelling Spirit we may know cleansing and victory and power to live a holy life.

Into the heart of his temple the Lord Jesus comes not only to occupy the throne, but to conquer and defeat the enemy.

If the *throne* speaks of his being Lord, the *soles of his feet* speak of his being conqueror.

If the *throne* speaks of his exercising authority, the *soles of his feet* speak of his defeating enemies.

If the *throne* speaks of his position, the *soles of his feet* speak of his activity.

These two aspects of his role must not be separated. They come together in two of the last statements of Jesus, spoken after his resurrection and before his ascension to the Father.

The first was spoken to his disciples on a hill in Galilee when he said: 'All authority in heaven and on earth has been given to me.' (Matthew 28:18) Some translations use the word 'power'. The original word is *exousia* which literally means power in the sense of authority. This is the power that belongs to a president or a king. It speaks of the position as King of Kings and Lord of Lords.

The other time Jesus spoke of power was to his disciples in Jerusalem immediately before his ascension when he said: 'You will receive power when the Holy Spirit comes on you.' (Acts 1:8) The word he used here was the word *dunamis*. From this we get such English words as *dynamic* and *dynamite*. It means power in the sense of sheer ability and force.

Now *exousia* and *dunamis* must be understood together. As I write this we have just witnessed a remarkable revolution in a country where the deposed President held absolute authority for more than twenty years. His word was law, and was ruthlessly carried out. In a very quick march of events, the people chose to obey no longer. They resisted his authority and he was powerless to do anything about it. He carried ultimate authority in that country, but when faced with such opposition he totally lacked the dynamism needed to exercise the authority. Within three days he stood trial refusing to recognize the court and claiming to be the President of the country and Commander in Chief of the armed forces, but he was a pathetic figure. Supposed authority, without the dynamic power to make it work, always is.

On the other hand there are those who know how to wield dynamic power, but who have no authority to do so, and they are dangerous! Take for example the various terrorist groups that exist throughout the world. They have plenty of dynamism, with the ability to actually make things happen, but no authority. Power that is not under authority is always dangerous.

What is needed is a combination of the authority to make decisions and issue orders, with the power to make sure they take place and actually happen.

Authority And Dynamic Power

Some years ago I travelled on an overnight bus from Glasgow to London. A few miles into the journey it became clear that one of the passengers on board was drunk. He was causing a nuisance to several other people, and after some complaints the driver pulled up on the side of the road, stopped the bus, walked up the aisle and asked the drunk man to get off and travel when he was sober. The man totally ignored him, and just looked out of the window. After several more requests which met with the same contempt, the driver returned to his seat in obvious defeat! We all felt a little sorry for him (though none of us had offered to manhandle the man off the bus!),and we set off down the road again. Presently we turned off the main road, drove in to a little town and pulled up outside a police station. The driver got out, then returned with two big Scottish policemen. The first told the drunk man that as he was disturbing the peace he was to leave the bus immediately. He was totally ignored. The policeman repeated his order at least once, perhaps twice, but with no response. Suddenly the policeman had his hand under the arm of the drunk man, he whisked him from his seat, swung him around to where his colleague hooked his arm under the man's other arm, and to the applause of the remaining passengers on the bus, they frog marched him up the steps of the police station, not to be seen by us again!

Now the driver had all the authority he needed to tell the man to get off the bus, but he lacked the power, and it was a little bit pathetic. The policemen had both the authority to order the man off the bus and the dynamism to make sure it happened, and it did!

When Jesus rose again from the dead he declared: 'All authority in heaven and on earth has been given to me.' He is King of Kings, Lord of Lords and has exclusive authority to tell you and I what to do. But that may seem to be very intimidating, for he may give me orders that I do not have the capability of performing! In fact, he probably will! But we must never detach the Lordship of Christ over our lives from the dynamism of the Holy Spirit within our lives. Jesus promised the disciples that it is when the Holy Spirit comes that they would receive power. Not power to go and do all kinds of things that may take their whim, but power exclusively to do what Christ as Lord commands them. When the Risen Lord gives us instructions it is the Holy Spirit within us who is the dynamic of God that makes them possible. The Lordship of Christ over us, and the dynamic presence of the Holy Spirit within us must never be detached in our understanding.

This comes together in the statement of Paul, 'The one who calls you is faithful and he will do it.' (1 Thessalonians 5:24) As God in Christ calls me to do something, so God the Spirit enables me to do it! That means there will never be any demand made upon me by the Lord Jesus Christ, that the Holy Spirit will not provide what is needed to get it done. Has God called you to some task for which you feel totally inadequate? Then if he has called you, the Holy Spirit will enable you. Do you find the demands of God in Scripture to be unrealistic? Then the Holy Spirit is the one who will make them work. Do you know what is right but cannot do it? Then you must trust the Holy Spirit to be your strength. The Lord Jesus Christ will never ever give you instructions for which the Holy Spirit is not totally adequate.

As the temple of God, your heart is not just the place of his throne, but the place of the souls of his feet, the place where he rules and conquers territory.

Watch The Entrances!

At one stage in Ezekiel's tour of the temple, he was brought to the front of the structure and told to listen very closely to an important regulation. 'Give attention to the entrance of the temple and all the exits of the sanctuary.' (Ezekiel 44:5) The Lord is in the temple. It has become the place of his throne, and the place where his feet have conquered. As a result his glory fills the place, but now he must be diligent in watching the entrances and exits, what comes in and what goes out.

The instruction to watch the entrance is a particularly important one. Earlier Ezekiel reports that 'The glory of the Lord entered the temple through the gate facing east' (Ezekiel 43:4) and it was then that his glory filled the temple. Now he is taken back to the same east gate and, 'The Lord said to me, "This gate is to remain shut. It must not be opened; no one may enter through it. *It is to remain shut because the Lord the God of Israel has entered through it.*" ' (Ezekiel 44:2)

As the Lord enters the temple the gate is to be shut, locked and never opened. There is no addition to the Lord himself, and any addition to him is really a subtraction from him. The extent to which I may want something more, is the extent to which I find him deficient. Paul wrote: 'Praise be to the God and Father of our Lord Jesus Christ, who has blessed us in the heavenly realms with *every spiritual blessing in Christ.*' (Ephesians 1:3) Peter also wrote: 'His divine power has given us *everything we need for life and godliness through our knowledge of him* who called us by his own glory and goodness.' (2 Peter 1:3) He is all that God is, and when we receive him we receive all God has for us. We must shut and bolt the door through which the Lord Jesus Christ has come. From within the Lord will have lots of things to do, but he has nothing more to bring from outside additional to himself.

I believe this is a particularly important word for our day. There seem many additions to Jesus on the Christian market at present. Any proclaimed need to *receive* what is not already in Christ, is a deception, and a particularly dangerous one at that. It is especially dangerous because anything I do receive that is not in Christ will become an enemy of Christ. Ezekiel records at this stage: 'This is what the Sovereign Lord says: No foreigner uncircumcised in heart and flesh is to enter my sanctuary,' (Ezekiel 44:9) and to 'the rebellious house of Israel' who had already done this, he says, 'you brought foreigners uncircumcised in heart and flesh into my sanctuary, desecrating my temple while you offered me food, fat and blood.' (Ezekiel 44:7) The *foreigners* who desecrated the temple were admitted whilst they offered the 'fat and blood' which were the requirements of Israel's worship. The enemy infiltrated the spiritual fibre of Israel because they were not discerned as being alien to it, and were in fact invited to participate in it!

At the moment of repentance and faith, we become indwelt by the Holy Spirit of God. 'If anyone does not have the Spirit of Christ, he does not belong to Christ. But if Christ is in you . . . your spirit is alive because of righteousness.' (Romans 8:9–10) It is the Spirit of Jesus whom we receive, and it is imperative that he is allowed to fill our lives. But he fills us from *within*, for he has already taken up residence within, as equally we may quench and grieve him from within. When we grieve him we do not drive him out, for the door has been shut. But as we do not drive him out when we offend him, we do not bring anything else in to please him, for there is nothing more to receive than him. Our responsibility is to let loose into every area of our lives the Spirit of God whom we have received at new birth.

The great strategy of Satan against the church is to make us dissatisfied with Christ. If he can cause us to hunger for something other than Christ he does not care what it might be. He does not care how good or beneficial it may seem to be, for any substitute for Christ becomes ultimately an enemy of Christ.

If I seek for experience as something in itself, if I seek for power, if I seek for some spiritual ecstasy, then Satan is prepared to hand it to me on a plate, clothed though it may be in evangelical language and enacted though it may be amidst the 'fat and blood' of God-ordained worship. It will not satisfy and will ultimately destroy. Only Christ will satisfy the heart. A feature of the door that remains open after Christ has entered, is that despite the infiltration of other new things, I will tire of them all, and like a drug whose potency has to be increased to keep pace with my growing capacity, I will need bigger and bigger spiritual kicks, and more bizarre expressions of ecstatic experience, until one day I throw in the towel, in disillusionment, or travel up some cul-de-sac that will rob me of the reality that should be mine in Christ. I do not believe this is an exaggeration of what is possible to any one of us, unless we bolt the door, for 'it is to remain shut because the Lord the God of Israel, has entered through it'. Will you guard the entrance, and keep it shut once the Lord Jesus has passed through to take his place in your heart?

Watch The Exits!

The last description Ezekiel gives in his vision is of the river that flowed out from the south side of the temple. (*See* Ezekiel 4:7) He followed a man with a measuring line and at intervals of five hundred yards he was led through the river. At first it was ankle deep, next it was knee deep, then it was up to the waist and after another five hundred yards it was so deep he could not pass through.

Along the river bank he saw a great number of trees. Their roots went into the water and they flourished and grew. Their leaves would not wither, their fruit would not fail and every month they would bear fresh fruit. The river ran its course down the mountain and into the Dead Sea, and as it entered the stagnant waters of that Sea, the water became fresh, the fish came alive and swarms of living creatures came to live around its shore. All of this, 'because the water from the sanctuary flows to them'.

What a beautiful picture of what flows out of the temple of God, 'and you are that temple'. (1 Corinthians 3:17) If we are to give careful attention to the entrances to the temple, we must certainly give attention to the exits. To have locked and bolted the entrances once the Lord has entered is so that what flows out will be from him and him alone. God has things to pour out through us into a world of great need, and he has chosen no channel but his people.

Jesus announced at the Feast in Jerusalem: 'If anyone is thirsty, let him come to me and drink. Whoever believes in me, as the scripture has said, streams of living water will flow from within him. By this he meant the Spirit.' (John 7:37–39) The plan for you and me is that we quench our thirst in Christ, not to be a sponge that soaks everything up so that we alone are the beneficiary, but to be a river that allows him to flow out through us to a thirsty, hungry, desperate world that needs to know Jesus for themselves.

I remember once flying across the land of India. From my window seat of the plane I was looking down on that vast country with its teeming population. At one stage, from our perspective of thirty-five thousand feet, the land below looked dry and barren, hardly able I imagined to maintain life at all, with no sign of any vegetation. Suddenly I saw a meandering strip of green stretching from the horizon and, as we came closer and flew across it, I saw a river running down the centre, bringing a narrow strip of vegetation and life to a dry burned land.

I wonder if that would be a picture of you? This is the image Jesus gave of the believer who has quenched his thirst in Christ and from whom there now flows a river of life. Philip Hacking in his contribution to the New

Keswick Collection Series, *What He Says, Where He Sends*, warns against becoming 'too introverted. The renewal of the life of the church must always be seen in renewed vision for evangelism . . . a renewed church will always be an outgoing church.' The result of guarding the entrances is that there will be something to see coming out of the exits! This is God's purpose for us, and the vision of Ezekiel was of a river whose effect must be that of the true and healthy Christian.

The River Was Fresh

Before commenting on the effect of the river, Ezekiel comments on the river itself. The influence of what we do will rarely exceed what we actually are ourselves! It is what we *are* that gives true effect to what we *do*. Jesus did not say to his disciples, 'You have the salt of the earth,' or 'You carry the light of the world.' He said 'You *are* the salt of the earth, You *are* the light of the world.' (Matthew 5:13–14) It is what we are that is the source of our effectiveness, and therefore what we are is always more important than what we do, for what we do is an expression of what we are.

The river was *fresh*! We looked in an earlier chapter at the fact that 'His mercies are new every morning.' (Lamentations 3:22–23) The Lord Jesus Christ is always ready to be to us today what we need today. He was not to us yesterday, what we need him to be to us today. He was then, what we needed yesterday. We do not need to live on stale experience or stale blessings, or stale provisions, but to keep in constant touch with him. It is this fresh walk with him that will make our work effective.

It has been said that things are better *caught* than *taught*. The people who have meant most in my life have *rubbed off* something on to me of which they are probably completely unaware. It derives from the freshness of their walk with God.

As the river entered the stagnant waters of the Dead Sea, its water too became fresh. Its freshness was contagious, and the Dead Sea is the most stagnant water in the world! The River Jordan flows in, but there is no outlet, for it is at the deepest point of the great Rift Valley, being something like 1,400 feet below sea level, the lowest point on the earth's surface. The hot sun causes the pure water to evaporate, the remaining sea growing ever more thick and stagnant with concentrated minerals and sediment. Do you see the significance of this? Of all the seas into which the river should flow, the Dead Sea would be the most difficult one to effect, yet it penetrates and changes it. This is the river that flows from the sanctuary of God and it is a picture of the potential of your life. Do not write off the difficult, tough, hardened people whom we would be tempted to think irredeemable, for 'where sin increased, grace increased all the more.' (Romans 5:20) God may pour you into the salty stagnant waters of some Dead Sea, and he will bring change!

The River Gave Life

The first result of the fresh flow of the river into the sea is that 'Swarms of living creatures will live wherever the river flows. There will be large numbers of fish.' There are no fish in the Dead Sea, it is impossible for them to live there in its natural condition. Here is a miracle of God, and it is a portrait of the Christian life.

God's purpose is to make a channel of his activity whereby he will raise the dead to life! This is the primary mission of Jesus: 'I have come that they may have life and have it to the full.' (John 10:10) Man's deepest need is not that he is guilty and needs to be forgiven, that he is lost and needs to know where he is going, but that he is dead and needs to come alive. Spiritual death is the absence of God from the human soul: 'As for you, you were dead in your transgressions and sins . . . separated from the life of God.' (Ephesians 2:1,4:18) Men and women, boys and girls who are lost, confused and dead in their sin, some having long given up hope of finding true meaning and life, will discover in us the very life of God and be given hope that they too might be brought to know him for themselves. He *is* the life. It is as people meet Christ in us, that their appetites may be awakened to search for him, for 'you will seek me and find me when you seek me with all your heart.' (Jeremiah 29:13)

The prime means through which the Lord Jesus Christ transmits his life and love, is through his people. There are probably few whose experience of finding Christ did not begin with an appetite created in their hearts through seeing the reality of Jesus Christ in other people. God will do it with you, however unwittingly on your part, for this is our privilege, this is our task, and this must be our confident expectation as we allow Christ to live his life in us and pour himself through us as 'a river of living water'.

The River Brought Fruit

Not only was there life in the sea, but fruit on the banks surrounding it. Jesus said to his disciples: 'I have chosen you and appointed you to go and bear fruit – fruit that will last.' (John 15:16) Fruit is never for the benefit of the one who bears it, but always for the benefit of others! Fruit bearing is not a badge of spirituality, but the means of serving others. In my book, *Christ For Real*,* I have written about the fact that God does not produce flowers of the Spirit in our lives, but the fruit of the Spirit. (*See* Galatians 5:22–23) There is a significant difference. Flowers are nice to look at, they make the dreary surroundings a little more pleasant, but they have little value beyond that. You do not use fruit for that purpose.

*Published by Marshall Pickering.

If a room is a little drab, you do not hang up a bunch of bananas to cheer it up! Fruit is not for decoration, it is for eating. It is for satisfying the hungry, for giving nourishment to the weary!

Christians exist for the benefit of others. Spiritual maturity can be measured in the contribution and input I bring to other people's lives. To be like Christ is not to adopt some pious pose, or to be experiencing an inner serenity which I do not want disturbed. It is to be getting my hands dirty in the interests of other people, and allowing them to feed on the fruit the Spirit produces in my life. The action on every page of the gospels is that of Jesus doing things for the benefit of others, and feeding them with his love, his joy, his patience and his goodness. Is there a river of love flowing out from your heart? A river of joy, of peace, of patience, of goodness, of kindness, of faithfulness, of gentleness, of self-control? These are the qualities Paul describes as the 'fruit of the Spirit'. These express the life of Jesus reproduced by the Holy Spirit within us, and then poured through us to others.

The River Got Deeper

Did you notice an interesting feature of the river, that flowed from the temple? The further it flowed, the deeper it got. After the first five hundred yards it was ankle deep, after one thousand it was knee deep, after fifteen hundred it was up to the waist and after two thousand yards it was too deep to cross.

In most spheres of life the effects of what we do decrease with time and distance. But that which derives from the activity of God within us gets deeper, richer and broader in its effects and repercussions. That is why *your* life, lived under the authority of Jesus Christ, empowered by his Holy Spirit, will always be significant.

Do you feel the river is fairly shallow as it flows out from within you? Well, maybe it seems that way. Perhaps you do not know a lot of people on whom you have had obvious and positive influence. Perhaps it seems very occasional that someone says 'thank you' for the enrichment you have brought to their lives. You cannot measure many direct answers to your prayer, or many people brought to Christ through your witness. The river seems very shallow, just as it did to Ezekiel! But go a few hundred yards, and amazingly it is deeper, go around the corner, it is deeper still, go down the hill and out of sight to the great Rift Valley and the river is getting fuller and deeper until you cannot pass through.

You do not have to know the *effect* of your life, you only have to know the *source* of your life. When you know the source is Christ, the effect is his responsibility! It will even look after itself, and you don't have to see it, for 'We walk by faith, not by sight.' (2 Corinthians 5:7)

When Ezekiel got down to the Dead Sea, the little ankle deep trickle he had walked through outside the temple up on the hill had become a life-giving river, bringing freshness and fruit wherever it went. What was the secret of this? He explains it very simply, 'because the water from the sanctuary flows to them.' (Ezekiel 47:12)

Do you remember what was happening in the sanctuary? The Lord was on the throne. He had occupied the territory. The entrance to the temple was closed to anything other than the Lord himself. The glory of God was filling the place, and from there the river of life began to flow. First it seemed a trickle, but soon a river, and the stagnant waters began to revive, the dead sea began to draw life and the barren trees began to bear fruit. And it was all God's doing!

11: These Found The Secret

God's temple on earth today is his people. This is where he lives, this is where we will meet him supremely. In the past his dwelling place was the tabernacle and Solomon's Temple. Then came the Second Temple built on Israel's return from the Babylonian Exile, enlarged and renewed by Herod in about 20BC, only to be destroyed by the Romans in AD70. By then his presence had not been in the Temple for forty years, for he had broken out the day Jesus Christ died on the cross. He now lives in the lives of people. The discovery of this fact has been the revolutionary point in the experience of many Christian people. Christ is our life, and it is in reliance upon him that we have the resources that enable us to live and function effectively.

Many notable men and women of God, whose ministry has had significant repercussions, trace the transformation of their Christian experience to this discovery.

Canon Harford-Battersby

Canon T.D. Harford-Battersby was the founder of the renowned Keswick Convention in 1875. The subsequent spontaneous growth in influence of the Convention has ranked it for decades as a world-wide movement, but its roots go back to a simple discovery by its founder, which transformed his personal life after years of spiritual barrenness. It was the discovery of the complete sufficiency of Jesus Christ, not only as his saviour from sin and death, but as the source of true spiritual life and power.

Canon Harford-Battersby was a minister in the Church of England, having already served the parish church in the town of Keswick, Cumbria, for twenty-four years. At the age of fifty-two, feeling 'burned out' in his ministry, he attended a conference in Oxford and heard Evan Hopkins speak on 'resting faith'. Shortly before, he had written that he was deeply conscious of the need of something fuller in his own life than he had yet experienced. His diary records: 'At this moment I am feeling much inward struggle . . . I feel that I am dishonouring God, and am wretched myself by living as I do.' He then prayed, 'God reveal to me the secret of this "more excellent way" and enable me to walk in it now and always.' Such was the attitude with which Canon Harford-Battersby attended the Oxford Conference, and the truth that he heard transformed his life. He wrote in his diary: 'Christ was revealed to me so powerfully and sweetly as the present Saviour in His all-sufficiency. I am His, and I do trust him to make good all His promises to my soul.' Several years later, speaking at the last Keswick Convention before he died, he referred to that time. 'I got a revelation of Christ to my soul, so extraordinary, glorious and precious, that from that day to this it illuminated my life. I found He was all I wanted; I shall never forget it; the day and hour are present with me. How it humbled me and what peace it brought.'

When asked about the permanent results of this discovery in his own life and that of others who shared it with him, he reported: 'The joy and peace to which so many bore testimony were indeed the fruit of the Spirit. In proportion as there has been faithfulness in guarding the treasure received, has it been productive of definite practical results. There are those who discovered a secret of power in service for Christ to which they were comparatively strangers, and their Christian life has flowed on mostly since with a sweet calm and inward peace which calls for continued thanksgiving.'*

Evan Hopkins

The man whose ministry had such profound effect on Canon Harford-Battersby at the Oxford Conference was Evan Hopkins. For many years Hopkins was acknowledged as the theologian of the Keswick movement, and his book, *The Law of Liberty In the Spiritual Life*, did more than anything else to explain the Convention to some evangelicals who were a little suspicious of it.

Evan Hopkins was a Church of England clergyman, but at the age of thirty-six, having been a Christian for thirteen years, he 'entered into a new experience of surrender and faith'. There is a written account of his wife's response to that occasion. 'How well I recall him coming home, deeply moved by what he had heard and experienced! He told me that he was like one looking out on a land wide and beautiful, flowing with milk and honey. It was to be possessed. It *was his!* As he described it all, I felt that he had received an overflowing blessing, far beyond anything that I knew; and it seemed as if a gulf had come between us. We sat up late that evening, talking, with our Bibles before us. Oh, I was hungry. At last, quite simply, but very really, I too took God at his word, and accepted Christ as my *indwelling Lord and life*, and believe that he did enthrone himself in my heart.'

Hopkins spoke at the first Keswick Convention in 1875 and for the following thirty-nine years without a break. At the last Convention he attended, in 1913, he looked back over the previous forty years and testified: 'I

---

* Various Keswick Convention memorabilia.

151

am privileged to testify that the blessing lasts. It has lasted with me for forty years. There have been many failures. I am not glorying in self, but what was revealed to me that day – *the all-sufficiency of Christ* – is as precious to my soul as it ever was.'*

Hudson Taylor

Hudson Taylor, well known as the pioneer missionary to China last century, whose life and principles of ministry have challenged and enriched many, and whose work led to the founding of the Overseas Missionary Fellowship, spent his first fifteen years in China utterly frustrated by his own failure to serve God effectively. It was then he discovered what he termed 'the exchanged life'. As he wholly surrendered his life to Christ, Christ gave his life wholly to him! Now it was not what he could do for Christ, but what Christ could do for him. A fellow missionary, John McCarthy, had written to him: 'It is not a striving to have faith, but a looking off to the Faithful One seems all we need; a resting in the Loved One entirely, for time and for eternity.' Taylor wrote: 'As I read I saw it all. I looked to Jesus, and when I saw – oh, how the joy flowed.' His fellow missionaries said of him: 'Mr Taylor went out, a new man in the world.' He wrote to his sister in England: 'As to work, mine was never so plentiful, so responsible, or so difficult; but the weight and the strain are all gone. The last month has been perhaps the happiest of my life; and I long to tell you what Christ has done for my soul.'†

---

* *So Great Salvation.* The History And Message Of The Keswick Convention by Steven Barabas. First published 1952. Marshall Morgan & Scott.
† Various sources. See *Hudson Taylor's Spiritual Secret* by Howard and Mary Taylor.

Oswald Chambers

Oswald Chambers is best known throughout the world for his classic daily devotional, *My Utmost For His Highest*, a volume almost certainly more widely read than any other book of its kind. Reading Chambers leaves an overwhelming impression that here is a man who knew God. He became a Christian whilst a boy, but years later when a student in Dunoon College, Scotland, despite the deep love he felt in his heart for the Lord Jesus Christ, he was aware 'I had no conscious communion with Him. The Bible was the dullest, most uninteresting book in existence.' He wrote, 'I was getting very desperate. I knew no one who had what I wanted; in fact I did not know what I did want. But I knew that if what I had was all the Christianity there was, the thing was a fraud. Then Luke 11.13 got hold of me – "If ye then, being evil, know how to give good gifts to your children, how much more shall your heavenly Father give the Holy Spirit to them that ask Him?"'

He described attending a meeting when a well-known lady (whom he does not name) spoke on this theme, and invited people to take God at his word and appropriate his indwelling presence. 'I felt nothing, but I knew emphatically my time had come. I had no vision of God, only a sheer dogged determination to take God at his word and to prove this thing for myself . . . I had no vision of heaven or of angels, I had nothing. I was as dry and empty as ever. Then I was asked to speak at a meeting and forty souls came to Christ. I was terrified and went to a friend and told him what had happened, and he said in effect, "Don't you remember claiming the Holy Spirit on the word of Jesus, and that He said, 'You shall receive power . . ?' This is the power from on high". Then like a flash, something happened inside me, and I saw that I had been wanting power in my own hand, so to speak, that I might say –

153

Look what I have by putting my all on the altar.

'If the four previous years had been hell on earth, these five years have truly been heaven on earth. Glory to God, the last aching abyss of the human heart is filled to overflowing with the love of God. After He comes in, all you see is "Jesus only, Jesus ever". When you know what God has done for you, the power and the tyranny of sin is gone and the radiant, unspeakable emancipation of the indwelling Christ has come.'

Andrew Murray

Andrew Murray, the South African Dutch Reformed minister and author of many books still popular today, made the same discovery ten years after becoming a Christian. He gave testimony of that time when speaking at the Keswick Convention in England in 1895. 'I was a minister, I may say, as zealous and as earnest and as happy in my work as anyone, as far as love of the work was concerned. Yet, all the time, there was burning in my heart a dissatisfaction and restlessness inexpressible. I remember in my little room in Bloomfontein, how I used to sit and think: "What is the matter? Here I am knowing that God has justified me in the blood of Christ, but I have no power in service." My thoughts, my words, my actions, my unfaithfulness – everything troubled me. Though all around thought me one of the most earnest of men, my life was one of deep dissatisfaction. I struggled and prayed as best I could. Through all these stumblings, God led me, without any very special experience that I can point to; but as I look back I do believe now that he was giving me more and more of his blessed Spirit.

'I can help you more by speaking not of any marked experience, but by telling very simply what I think God has given me now, in contrast to the first ten years of my Christian life.

'In the first place, I have learned to place myself before God every day, as a vessel to be filled with the Holy Spirit. He has filled me with the blessed assurance that he, as the everlasting God, has guaranteed his own work in me. If there is one lesson I am learning day by day it is this: that it is God who worketh all and in all. Oh, that I could help any brother or sister to realise this! I will tell you where you fail. You have never yet heartily believed that he is working out your salvation. The everlasting God is working out the image of his Son in you.

'You will ask me, "Are you satisfied? Have you got all you want?" God forbid. With the deepest feeling of my soul I can say I am satisfied with Jesus now; but there is also the consciousness of how much fuller the revelation can be of the exceeding abundance of his grace. May he teach us our own nothingness and transform us into the likeness of his Son, and help us to go out and be a blessing to our fellow-men. Let us trust him and praise him in the midst of a consciousness of our own utter unworthiness, and in the midst of a consciousness of failure and of remaining tendency to sin. Not withstanding this, let us believe that our God loves to dwell in us; and let us hope without ceasing in his still more abundant grace.'*

The history of Christianity is full of such testimonies to a discovery of the complete sufficiency of Christ, usually born out of a sense of despair, and to the inner working of his Holy Spirit in the lives of the witnesses as the subsequent source of all power, fruitfulness and effectiveness.

Luis Palau

Luis Palau, known throughout the world for his evangelistic ministry in our own day, records in his autobiography the time he came to the end of his own resources and

* The Keswick Week, 1895.

discovered Jesus Christ to be all that he had been trying to be on his own. Recording the content of a message given by Major Ian Thomas to students in Portland, Oregon, he writes: 'Thomas told of many Christian workers who failed at first because they thought they had something to offer God. I thought, "That's exactly my situation. I am at the end of myself." When Ian Thomas closed with Galatians 2:20, it all came together. "I have been crucified with Christ; it is no longer I who live, but Christ who lives in me; and the life I now live in the flesh I live by faith in the Son of God who loved me and gave himself for me" (RSV). You can't imagine the complete release I felt as a result of that little chapel talk. Years of searching had come to an end. There would be many, many more problems that had to be worked out on the basis of the principle in Galatians 2:20, but my biggest spiritual struggle was finally over. I would let God be God and Luis Palau be dependent on him. I ran back to my room in tears and fell to my knees next to my bunk. I prayed: "Lord, now I get it, I understand. The whole thing is 'not I, but Christ in me.' It is not what I'm going to do for you, but rather what you're going to do through me."' Later Palau adds: 'It was thrilling to finally realise that we have everything we need when we have Jesus Christ literally living in us. Our inner resources are God himself, because of our union with Jesus Christ. He wanted me not to depend on myself, but on Christ alone, the indwelling, resurrected, almighty Lord Jesus.'*

Paul: When Weakness Is Strength

Failure is so often the prelude to discovering that the ability to survive and live is found in Christ himself. The apostle Paul records his own experience of this. To the

* *The Luis Palau Story*, as told by Jerry B. Jenkins, pp. 134-5.

Corinthians Paul catalogues a list of qualities and experiences about which he could legitimately boast, but then into his life comes a 'messenger of Satan to torment me'. He does not explain exactly what he is talking about, except that it rendered him weak. It was precisely here that he discovered power. 'Three times I pleaded with the Lord to take it away from me. But he said to me "My grace is sufficient for you, for my power is made perfect in weakness." Therefore I will boast all the more gladly about my weaknesses, so that Christ's power may rest on me . . . For when I am weak, then am I strong' (2 Corinthians 12:7-10).

No one can ever be too weak for Christ to work in them and through them, but they can be too strong. No one can be too simple, but they can be too clever. No one can ever be too poor, but they can be too rich. The danger when we feel strong is that we believe it! It is as God exposes to us our weakness that we are ready to trust him for a strength that is not our own. It is for this reason that Paul later states: 'We are weak . . . yet by God's power we will live . . . to serve you', and again, 'We are glad whenever we are weak' (2 Corinthians 13:4,8). It is our sense of strength that becomes our weakness and our sense of weakness that becomes our strength. The extent of my strength is the measure of my self-sufficiency which will become, in turn, the cause of my barrenness. Conversely, it will be the extent of my weakness that will become the measure of my dependency on God which will become the cause of my fruitfulness. Hence Paul's affirmation: 'We are glad whenever we are weak'!

When God looked for people to use, Paul also reminded the Corinthians that, 'Not many of you were wise by human standards; not many were influential; not many were of noble birth. But God chose the foolish things of the world to shame the wise; God chose the weak things of the world to shame the strong. He chose the lowly things of this world and the despised things – and the things that are not – to nullify the things that are, so that no one may boast before him. It is because of him that you are in Christ Jesus, who has become for us wisdom from God – that is, our righteousness, holiness and redemption. Therefore as it is written: "Let him who boasts boast in the Lord"' (1 Corinthians 1:26-31).

If any credit is to be given it belongs exclusively to God. His power is displayed in people who know they cannot take responsibility for it themselves. Some in Corinth were taking themselves, or their leaders, far too seriously. Some of them were claiming to be of Paul, some of Apollos, and some of Peter, as though these men held some responsibility for their spiritual life, or were somehow free to market their own brand of Christianity, of which you could take your pick!

Paul asks indignantly: 'What after all is Apollos? And what is Paul? Only servants through whom you came to believe. I planted the seed, Apollos watered it, but God made it grow. So neither he who plants nor he who waters is anything, but only God' (1 Corinthians 3:5-7). It is not to the servant but to the Lord himself that we give credit, and from whom we derive our resources. That is why the true servant of God never leads people to become dependent upon himself, but always to become dependent upon God. To bring people to a dependency upon myself might make them easier to handle and ensure I can get my plans implemented with little fuss, but I have created a cult. It may be founded on sound orthodox theology but I have never taken people beyond spiritual babyhood to a healthy, wholesome maturity in Christ.

In the spiritual life of others it is dependency upon God that is our goal. I may play a role in their coming to birth and in the establishing of them in the Lord Jesus Christ. But the sooner I wean them from myself and bring them to a place of dependency upon God, the sooner I will introduce them to spiritual maturity and usefulness. The goal must be independence of myself and dependency upon God. We must always relate to each other in mutual respect and mutual submission, but we acknowledge only one Lord, Christ himself, and only one source of strength, Christ himself.

We must never be afraid of letting people discover their own weakness. To fail is almost certainly to grow. We cannot really teach it to others, for though they may seem to understand it as a proposition, they will need to learn it ultimately in their own experience. It has been when people discover their own inherent weakness that again and again God has broken in with the revelation of his strength. This has been true not only in Scripture but throughout the history of the Christian Church, and lies at the root of almost any great work and movement of God.

Some years ago, Dr V. Raymond Edman, then President of Wheaton College in Illinois, wrote a book entitled, *They Found The Secret*. The book looks at twenty people who have made marked impact for God, some of previous generations and some of recent and current times. In his introduction he makes an interesting observation: 'The details of their experiences are usually quite different; yet as we listen to their stories and watch their lives, either in our reading or in our contact with them, we begin to see a pattern which reveals their secret. Out of discouragement and defeat they have come into victory. Out of weakness and weariness they have been made strong. Out of ineffectiveness and apparent uselessness they have become efficient and enthusiastic.

'The pattern seems to be: self-centredness, self-effort, increasing inner dissatisfaction and outer discouragement, a temptation to give it all up because there is no better way; and then finding the Spirit of God to be their

159

strength, their guide, their confidence and companion –
in a word, their life.'

What Has Happened So Far?

As I conclude this book, my young daughter has come in
to my study to ask: 'What has happened so far?' She
thinks I have written a story. Maybe I have. Maybe you
have seen glimpses of your own life mirrored in these
pages, for I have been telling your story. May I ask you
her question: 'What has happened so far?'

We neither want nor need to imitate another person's
experience, nor reduce God's dealings with them to a
pattern that we would superimpose on ourselves or anyone else. When we look for a pattern God normally sur-
prises us by dealing with us in unexpected ways. But if
you are 'burned out' like Harford-Battersby, 'at the end
of myself' like Luis Palau, 'utterly frustrated' like Hudson
Taylor, with 'no conscious communion with God' like
Oswald Chambers, or feeling 'deep dissatisfaction' like
Andrew Murray, then you must get hold of the principle
that lies behind every expression of effective Christianity.
It is Christ as our *Lord* who directs us, and we live in submission to his authority, and obedience to his commands.
But it is his Spirit as our *Life* who enables us. He is our
power and strength, and we trust him, stepping out into
every new day and every new situation with the conviction that the One whom we obey, is totally able by his
indwelling Holy Spirit to accomplish his purposes.

If this is not yet your story, whatever you have been,
wherever you have been, as a child of God you are a new
creation in Christ. He has planned your future, and all
the resources you will ever need are available in the Lord
Jesus Christ. Step out with confidence in him, and
together you shall make it happen.